CW01461163

Lessons and Beliefs

Learning to Love

by Mark Tedesco

Academia Publications

Copyright © 2024 by Mark Tedesco
Copyright © 2024 Academia Publications
All rights reserved. No part of this book may be used or reproduced
or transmitted to any form or by any means, electronic or mechanical,
including photocopying, recording, or by any information and retrieval
system, without written permission from the Publisher.

Lessons and Beliefs: Learning to Love - Mark Tedesco

Editor: Katherine Boyle

III. Edition: September 2024

Library of Congress Cataloging-in Publication Data
Mark Tedesco
ISBNs:
Softcover: 979-8-33036-52-0-3
eBook: 979-8-33036-52-1-0

1. Love 2. Memoir 3. LGBTQ+
© Academia Publications

To John

Lessons and Beliefs

Learning to Love

by Mark Tedesco

Table of Contents

Introduction

Searching for love can be challenging because it is often unmarked territory, influenced by popular culture and conscious or unconscious convictions. This book is the fruit of reflecting on beliefs tried by experience. Rather than adopting a set of external standards, the lessons learned can become one's greatest teacher.

My own quest began when I walked into a bar in Washington, D.C. one day and met the one who I thought was the companion of my dreams. Rather than being the end of this search, it was only its inception. Each time I believed that I had found true love, it turned out to be ephemeral.

I began to ask myself what beliefs I was bringing into my relationships. How were these beliefs confirmed, negated, or did they evolve? Which components constituted lasting friendships and healthy relationships?

This book is the story of my own search as I carry the reader along as we examine beliefs held and lessons learned from each significant bond. Though my own experience is in the gay world, the wisdom gained is universal.

New lessons will be learned along this journey, which I hope will be fruitful to others on this path.

Chapter 1: The School of First Love

First love is only a little foolishness and a lot of curiosity.
George Bernard Shaw

Beliefs:
Being gay means being less of a man.
Love is enough to make a relationship work.
The abundance of love in one partner can compensate for its lack in the other.

Part I: Falling in Love with Masculinity

I had never been in love before, and I had no idea how such a thing felt, much less how it looked. I didn't know what a healthy love, which builds one up, and an unhealthy love, which tears one apart, consisted of. I didn't even know I was looking for love until I met Rocco.

Having been in the seminary in Rome, I was shielded from, but fascinated by, gay life. I was studying theology, living in Washington, D.C., and pursuing a doctorate when I first walked into The Eagle on a cold, winter Saturday night. It was a dark place, a leather bar, which tended to draw a manly and mature crowd. The place smelled of urine, the music was pounding, and the drinks were flowing.

I stopped inside the door and looked around. I felt self-conscious and uncomfortable. Spotting the stairs on my right, I began to climb them to get out of the spotlight. When I was halfway up, I glanced down and saw a muscular, African-American man with a handsome, bearded face behind the bar. He looked at me and nodded. I nervously nodded back and fled up the stairs.

The second floor was darker, the crowd less pretty, and the music was pounding even louder. To fit in, I ordered a draft beer and leaned against the wall, sipping the bitter brew. Not being much of a drinker, I was soon lost in my thoughts, wondering about this man I just saw below. Who was he? What was he like? What was behind that handsome face?

I had not even come to terms with the fact that I was homosexual. My only exposure to gay men had been to more effeminate types. Because I did not relate to them, I figured I must not be gay, but something else. I didn't know what that something was, but I told myself I was in some stage I would pass through.

My beer was finished, and I could not stomach another. What if I went downstairs and introduced myself to this man? Shook his hand, showed interest, and got to know him? I wavered because I felt shy and intimidated by this place. I finally pulled myself off the wall and went down the stairs to take the plunge. As I turned toward the bar, however, the man was engrossed in a conversation with some customers; he did not look up. I did not hesitate or linger but went out the door, into my car, and home to my tiny studio apartment near the Catholic University in D.C.

I was drawn to the foul-smelling bar the next

night in the hope that I might see this man again. It was a special event, "underwear night," on which the bartenders wore little, and patrons were encouraged to do so also. I decided to keep my clothes firmly on. I was dismayed when I sighted another bartender working. Many people were heading up the stairs. I soon discovered the real party: a stage, an MC, and three or four bartenders. Then I saw him—busy serving drinks, bare-chested in his skivvies, leaning over to hear the customer's orders. I sat at the far end of the bar and ordered a beer.

I sat for a while, observing. I noticed that this man made eye contact with his customers. He often laughed, exchanged a joke, and to some, gave a kiss. He was busy but showed no signs of stress and seemed to enjoy his work. I looked him up and down; he was a real man, one hundred percent, oozing masculinity from across the room.

As the evening wore on, the place got busier, and some type of underwear contest began. I looked around at the crowd, some in undies, others fully dressed like me. I felt a bit uncomfortable.

It was not a good evening to make personal contact with the object of my interest, so I slipped out and returned to my world again.

During the day, I was carrying a full load of studies. I lived in a studio apartment near Catholic University, but I kept my religious background in the closet as I explored the gay world. I was hurrying to get through my homework so that I could drive over to The Eagle to try to meet this man.

It was 8 p.m. on a Tuesday when I pulled up, and the bar was almost empty. I didn't see my bartender downstairs, so I went up and found him tending to only one customer. I sat down nervously, and my palms began to sweat: "What can I do you for?" he cheerfully asked me as he walked over.

"Draft is fine," was my reply. As he served me, he reached over to shake my sweaty hand. "I'm Rocco," he said. I liked him. We began to chat. He told me of his past and that he had a son. I told him I was from California and was here on a scholarship. "What are you studying?" he asked. "Education," I replied, not ready to reveal more.

Rocco was articulate, charming, and sexy. "When will you come to see me again?" he asked, as I made ready to go. I had to be in class the following day.

"Are you working tomorrow?" I asked.

"Yes."

"Till tomorrow then," I said as I shook his hand and left.

Coming to The Eagle became my nightly routine for the next two weeks, after my studies and dinner. At each visit, I revealed a little bit more of myself and Rocco of himself. "I'm retired navy," he said. "I spent fourteen years in the military. I was also married and have a son. My ex-wife told me she was using birth control, but I think she got pregnant to try to keep me," he explained. I asked how old his son was. "Fourteen or fifteen, I think," he said. They were not close. At that time, I did not stop to ask myself what this ignorance of his own son's age meant about Rocco's character.

"I have a partner," he disclosed a week after we met. "He is in the Marine Corps Band. He travels a lot and is out of town for the next month. His name is William." It didn't bother me in the least that Rocco was not single. I was not looking for a relationship. Or so I told myself.

"Mark, would you walk me home after work today? I get off early, and I can show you where I live. I rent a room from my friend Harry, and he has a big house around the corner." My heart leaped at the possibility of becoming more bonded with this Rocco. It was around 7 p.m. that we went to his house, a large, dilapidated Victorian; upon entering, I was struck by the strong dog odor. "How about a beer?" Rocco asked as he went to the kitchen. What was it about this man that I found so attractive? He did not fit the stereotype of being gay that I had been exposed to. He looked and acted like a man; he fully embraced his masculinity, and he didn't see that as a contradiction to being gay. Rocco represented that possibility for me: if this is what gay can mean, then I can be that, too.

I was lost in these thoughts when he brought back the beer and sat next to me on the sofa. Rocco was suddenly more affectionate and put his arm around me. The front door creaked and began to open; he quickly withdrew his arm and scooted away. A redheaded, bearded man walked in, about 45 years old, average build, blue jeans, flannel shirt. "Welcome home, Harry," Rocco said as he shifted uncomfortably. "This is Mark," and I stood and shook Harry's hand. "Harry and I are housemates," Rocco explained. There was awkwardness after greeting each other, so Harry retreated upstairs, and I remained with Rocco.

The atmosphere had changed. I finished my beer and said, "I'll see you tomorrow at the bar," and I left.

Meeting and getting to know Rocco was helping me to change my feelings about being gay. If I could embrace being gay and be fully a man at the same time, then I would not feel the shame that I had carried. Perhaps this was why I felt so drawn to him so much that driving across D.C. in traffic to see him seemed more a gift than a burden.

My nightly visits continued until a few days later when he invited me to his out-of-town partner's place. "It is across from the Marine barracks. Meet me over there at eight o'clock tomorrow," he told me at the bar as he winked. We both knew what the unspoken plan was. I couldn't wait to break the sexual barrier with him.

The following weekend this encounter did indeed take place. We decided instead to meet at the bar as he ended his shift. Because his partner was not around, we would go to his house to spend some intimate time together. My heart raced as we left The Eagle, and I followed Rocco in my car.

William lived in a simple, one-bedroom townhouse. I was offered a beer, and I accepted because it seemed like the right thing to do. Maybe I will develop a taste for this stuff, I thought to myself. We made small talk for a few minutes. "Would you like to see a picture of William?" he asked.

"Sure."

As I looked, he pulled a photo out; I hid my surprise at his choice for a partner. William was small, thin, and very average-looking. Rocco was big, muscular, imposing, and handsome. "He has a good heart," Rocco said, reading my thoughts. He continued, "He calls me Papa." Because I was so new to the gay world,

I did not know whether to consider this odd or not. "I need to call William now, so you need to be very quiet. I don't want him to know I have company," he said. When he made his call, I took the opportunity to go to the bathroom. Without thinking, I flushed the toilet, and Rocco jumped out of his seat and walked toward the bathroom. He motioned with his hand for me to be quiet, and I overheard him say to William, "I'm just going to the bathroom here while we're talking." When he got off the phone, I apologized for not thinking, but Rocco said William didn't seem phased by it.

He then took me by the hand and led me to the back bedroom, where he kissed me. I had so few sexual experiences until that time that simply an embrace would almost make me explode, but I wanted this to last. As we lost our clothes and tumbled onto the bed, I wanted to possess this man and for him to possess me. He was a man to the core, and this was an incredible turn-on for me. I wanted to be one with him, but it didn't seem the right moment. Both of us were happy and satisfied when all was over.

I felt overwhelmed by the experience with Rocco. I had never felt this way before. After holding each other for some time, Rocco suggested we return to the sofa to talk for a bit. "Mark, I'm a top. I like to fuck, but I do not get fucked. I like to be inside a man, and I would love to do that with you. But I see you getting nervous now, so I wouldn't force it, but when you are ready... As you saw, I'm pretty big down there. When William saw it, he said, 'No way is that thing getting inside me!' but I helped him work up to it until he can take it fine now." He stopped and looked at me. I had no intention of letting anyone inside. I wanted to flee. Rocco changed the direction of the conversation. "I'd like you to meet William. It would be easier for me if we could all be friends. When he is back here in a few weeks, let's have a drink together." I nodded, and he continued: "It's getting late, and I gotta get up for work. Will I see you tomorrow?"

"For sure," I replied, and we kissed once more before I left.

My belief that being homosexual equaled diminished manhood was being chipped away by my contact with Rocco. He exemplified the fullness of manhood, yet there was not a heterosexual bone in his body! Another way began to open up for me, a way of being in my own skin that felt comfortable, that felt like home. Something was being revealed in this experience that felt right.

When Rocco closed the door, walking toward my car, I looked up at the Marine Barracks again. It was the same building, but everything seemed different. I couldn't yet put my finger on what had changed.

Part II: First Love

Over the next week, I discovered that the sexual encounter with Rocco stoked my emotions until I was on fire. He became the emotional center of my day, and I began to dread his partner William's return. I called Rocco several times in the weeks that followed, but he rarely picked up the phone, and he never returned calls. "I'm not a phone person," he explained on one of my bar visits. I soon learned that the best way to communicate with him was to go to The Eagle when there were few patrons or show up just as he was getting off his shift

18

because he would always sit and drink before going home. I sat next to him one night and felt an emotional connection that I had never sensed before.

The dreaded day soon arrived, and William returned to D.C. Rocco asked me to meet him at the bar and suggested I ask William out for a movie to establish a friendship, hoping that no suspicion might arise.

Rocco was working behind the bar while William was sitting on a stool; when I walked in, they both turned. "Mark, this is William," he said, and I extended my hand. William was even smaller than he appeared in the photo, almost like a boy. Average build, average face. I didn't get it. I sat down next to him and engaged in small talk for a few minutes until Rocco walked away.

"So how did you and Rocco meet," he asked. Did I sense suspicion in his tone?

"Here at the bar. I'm new in town, so Rocco made me feel comfortable." Did William feel threatened by me, I wondered?

"William, would you like to do a movie sometime? I don't have any friends in town, and it would be nice to do that with you because Rocco is always working." William agreed, and we settled on a date and time the following Saturday.

Things were different when I went to the bar over the next few days. Rocco was not accessible. He could not reach over the bar and hug me in case William would walk in. If I came at the end of his shift, William was already seated there; he knew the routine as well. William became very clingy toward Rocco when I was present as if claiming his territory. By the time Saturday rolled around, I had no desire to go to the movies with him but already felt obligated.

After the movie, we went out for a bite and kept the whole conversation light. William didn't seem to be interested in me, my background, or who I was, so I focused on him. He told me about his family, his love for Rocco, his work for the Marine Corps band, and his life in D.C. The point of all this was to allay William's fears so that the three of us could hang out together without any awkwardness. That is what Rocco wanted. That is not what I wanted. My feelings for Rocco had gone beyond that.

Love turned to suffering as my access to Rocco diminished. There were times when we had a few minutes alone, and he began to confide in me some of the issues he had in his relationship with William. This made me start to hope that perhaps, someday, I would have a chance with Rocco. But I would never instigate this.

Weeks turned to months, and the holiday season soon arrived. I had four weeks off from school, so I decided to return home to my parents' house for three weeks. It was painful to leave Rocco, but somehow, going home seemed the right thing to do.

I was involved with the Catholic Church. When I arrived home, I was expected to resume some parish activities during Christmastime because I worked for the Catholic diocese and was on a scholarship.

Everyone at home that I encountered treated me as if I were the same person I was six months earlier, but I felt completely different. It was as if I were masquerading as this person I no longer was; I was an impostor. It only took me one day to realize that I could not stay for three weeks.

20

I missed Rocco terribly. Though the fact that he had a partner caused me sorrow, my life back in Sacramento was no longer my life.

My mother passed away when I was a child, and I had always been close to her. I turned to her in this circumstance and drove to the cemetery where she was buried. There I opened my heart to ask her for her help. After putting some flowers on her grave, I told her the whole story of Rocco and my emotional mess. "Please, mom," I pleaded, "Pray, find a way that Rocco and I might be together someday! Please." This desire had grown so much in my heart that it began to consume me.

I had never been in love before, and the feelings were so new and unique; I became convinced that my happiness was dependent on whether I ended up with Rocco or not. I could not identify what Rocco and I had in common, what connection there was between us, other than a feeling. As I drove over the hill from my parents' house toward some shops, I was aware of new sentiments that seemed so intense that no one else would be able to understand them. They seemed bigger than me.

Life at home with family and friends became unbearable. As I lay in bed one night, turning these things over and over again in my head, I reached a decision: I would return early, cutting this vacation short. I would tell my family that I needed to go back early to work on a paper. In this way, I could continue my new life. That is exactly what I did.

I arrived back in D.C. and landed a job at a non-profit organization. I then found a small house to rent over by The Eagle and around the corner from Rocco.

All these changes happened within the course of a few weeks.

I told Rocco about my new job. "Are they hiring?" he asked. Yes, they were because they were starting a call center and were interviewing anyone with a bachelor's degree.

"Would you like me to set you up with an interview?"

Rocco said, "Yes." Were my prayers being answered?

There were various clubs affiliated with The Eagle in D.C. whose purpose was fraternization and fundraising for gay causes. One such club had only one meeting per year, and its theme was the animal kingdom. Each member had to be inducted and was given an animal name that somehow reflected his appearance or personality. Rocco's nickname was Angus, like a black bull. Rocco invited me to the event on the upper floor of The Eagle, at which over fifty members were present. I was not inducted because I knew few people so far.

I had made some friends in the city, and I was closest to Victor and Barry, a couple who had been together for twelve years. They both had a sense of humor, and when I told them about the club meeting, Victor asked, "Was William there?" (They had met William at the bar on several occasions.) I thought a minute and nodded. Victor continued: "I could guess what name they gave him. William the Weasel! He's a weasel!"

Ever since Weasel had returned home, Rocco and William's relationship had become more volatile. The Weasel was very insecure and jealous and would often stealthily enter the home where Rocco lived, creep up the stairs, and surprise him in his room. He was making sure Rocco was not with someone else.

He also popped into the bar at unexpected times and wanted all of Rocco's attention when he was serving customers. It sounded like a disintegrating situation, but I said nothing.

Strangely, by plan or coincidence, Rocco was hired by the same organization as I was. Our lives were becoming more intertwined.

Weeks passed, and Weasel's behavior was becoming more and more erratic. He was displeased that Rocco and I were working together. For my part, I stayed away from that whole situation, but it was evident that Rocco was getting fed up. "I told William I need a break," he said one evening after he finished his shift. "I told him not to come to the bar anymore or to show up at the house." I nodded.

"What do you think is going to happen?" I asked. Rocco shrugged.

It was only two days later that I found Rocco at the bar, with an exhausted look on his face. "What's wrong?" I asked.

"William came over again; he just showed up in my room, so we had it out. We had a huge argument. We broke up. So that's that," he said. I was sad for this suffering and hoped I had not caused it.

"I hope it was not me," I finally said. Rocco shook his head.

"No, it's not you. This started way before you came along, Mark." I was relieved. We began to talk about work and decided to meet up the following morning to walk there together.

I showed up at Rocco's house five minutes early the following day, but he was not ready. By the time he had his coat and tie on, it was fifteen minutes before clock-in time. We practically had to run to get to work on time, and we were both sweating heavily as we walked in the front door with one minute to spare. This would become an almost daily occurrence with Rocco, which annoyed me. When we spoke about it, he promised to be ready on time, but it never happened. I kept my frustration to myself.

Walking to work, eating lunch, and going to the gym together after work, we were spending more time together than ever. Within that first week of work, we became sexual again, and Rocco began coming to my place almost every evening. He was going to The Eagle less. "Do you miss the bar?" I asked after dinner.

"Why should I miss it? I have everything I need," he said as he hugged me.

As we settled into this routine, it was as if my prayers to my mother had been answered.

At work, everyone saw us as close friends. Though Rocco was fearful of being known as gay in the workplace, most of the men working at the call center were gay, and many of the administrative staff were former priests. I began to make some new friendships there.

One morning I left the house to go to work and noticed something different about my car. I went to inspect it more closely and saw that the windshield had been bashed in. Who would do such a thing, I wondered? When I met Rocco at his house later and told him about it, he paused and nodded. "You know Mark, it might have been William." I wondered if I could feel safe with that little man prowling around.

Rocco slept over that following Friday, but when I got up in the middle of the night to go to the bathroom, he was not in bed. I went downstairs, and he was not there either. He had left. Had I said or done something to offend? Had he taken ill? Was he in the hospital? I returned to bed, unsure of what had happened. But I could no longer sleep. The following day I called him, and he picked up the phone. "Are you OK?" I asked. "Yeah, I just couldn't sleep, so I came home to my bed." I was relieved. "As long as you're OK," I replied. But something bothered me about the whole incident. "I'll be working at the bar later if you want to stop by," he said.

I reflected later that day about what annoyed me. It was not the fact that Rocco left, but that he didn't tell me he was leaving. I didn't want to be left wondering, but I was hesitant to bring it up because I didn't want to make waves. "Mark, if you don't communicate your feelings, it will build resentment," my friend Thomas from California advised me.

It was a struggle for me to be open with my feelings with Rocco because I feared I would alienate him, but I knew I would be stewing unless I did. A few days later, I asked him just to let me know if he needed to leave during the night so I wouldn't wonder. "But I didn't want to wake you up," he objected.

"I'd rather be woken up than sit there and wonder if you are OK." We reached an agreement, and I felt better that I had expressed what I felt.

As the weeks passed, we settled into a routine of work, gym, grabbing a bite for dinner, saying good night, and then going to our respective houses. On weekends, Rocco worked at the bar and then usually came to sleep at my place.

One day, the routine was broken as we walked home

from work and passed in front of The Eagle. Rocco stopped in front and announced, "I need a drink." I paused to decide what I wanted to do. I had spent a lot of time at the bar to be with Rocco; starting to go after work would take away my gym time, the time I set aside to take care of myself. Rocco inched toward the door.

"No, I need to get to the gym," I said.

"OK," he said as he ducked inside. I stood there for a minute before continuing. Something inside of me told me that this was the beginning of the end. I had so little in common with this man; my need to love was so intense that it blinded me to the differences. But as soon as that thought became conscious, I quashed it.

Rocco's stops at the bar became a nightly routine, and sometimes I compromised, remaining with him so we could have some time together. But because I was not much of a drinker, sitting on a bar stool for hours bored me. I soon became restless.

We were different, but I was still completely immersed in this feeling for Rocco. My friends teased me about it; others wondered out loud whether this person was good for me. But I was convinced. When my friend Victor asked me about my relationship, I replied, "I can't even imagine my life without Rocco!" I was smitten. Love was enough to overcome all the differences between us, or so I thought.

Months passed, and our work routine continued, but Rocco spent more and more time at The Eagle. On Fridays, he would be tired from work, so he would sleep in his own bed after spending several hours drinking alone. He said he rested better that way. He worked the Saturday and Sunday daytime shifts and afterward sat at the bar, nursing a drink, often till closing at 2 a.m. I would stay with him because otherwise, I would not have another opportunity. I didn't mind this at first because I figured that he would grow out of this. He just needs to settle into his new relationship; he will change, I thought. I awaited this change with loyalty.

The care-taking role came naturally for me, so I began to make Rocco dinners and snacks and carry them to the bar when he was on shift. It was an opportunity, outside of work, to visit and feel close to him. Taking care of someone gave me a feeling of intimacy. On one such visit, I asked him what else he liked to do besides hanging out at The Eagle. "I just like it here. I feel safe," he replied.

"What about going to the movies or out to eat?" I asked.

"Sure. You arrange it, and I'll be there." So, I arranged a trip to the movies at a local mall for the following Saturday.

When I got to the bar to pick Rocco up, he was sitting, sipping his drink. "Are you ready?" I asked.

"I just need to relax for a while," was his reply. So, I pulled up a stool next to his. I had the impression that he lost interest in the movie.

"Do you want to go?" I asked.

"I told you I would go. I'm tired, but yes, let's go."

"We're going to miss it unless we get going." He gulped his drink and reluctantly got up.

The movie was Forrest Gump, and during the film, Rocco cried and cried. When we walked out into the mall, I asked him why. "It reminded me of you," he said, with no further explanation.

In the weeks that followed, I began to think of more

creative things that Rocco and I could do together: a live show, the natural history museum, or dinner out. Each time it was like pulling teeth. The only thing he seemed to enjoy was sitting in a dark bar sipping on a drink for four, five, or six hours.

Weekday mornings, Rocco and I continued to meet at his place; he was never ready, and we always had to rush to arrive at work on time. After work, it was the same; I waited in front of the building for him to put his desk in order before leaving. After eight hours on the job, I was always eager to leave and get on with my personal life. I grew impatient waiting for Rocco, night after night. On one of these occasions, I grew so impatient that I decided to slowly begin to walk home, often glancing back to let him catch up. He never appeared. When I met him the following day, he was upset that I had left him. "I will wait up to twenty minutes for you before leaving. I start to get irritated after that, but I don't want to be irritated at you. So, I will wait, but if you get held up, I will start to head home." He agreed though he seemed unhappy with my new boundary.

A year had passed since Rocco and I had gotten together, and our job situation had changed. He got a promotion to supervisor and me to the Help Desk. These promotions changed our hours, so we no longer walked to and from work together, thereby eliminating the tension. The schedule change made contact with Rocco more challenging; I started to feel that I was doing all the work to spend time together.

I created some friendships of my own, and on Thursdays, we began to meet at another bar to talk and enjoy ourselves. It was at one of these Thursday get-togethers that a friend of mine, Barry, gave me some information about Rocco that I did not want to hear. "Mark, Rocco is playing around behind your back. I saw him in the bar tongue-kissing a guy, and after his shift, they left together. This Rocco is not what he seems...." His voice trailed off, and he looked at me. I was shocked into disbelief, and my whole emotional state began to crumble. Barry observed this. Then he stopped and put his hand on my shoulder. "Mark, I'm kidding." I was relieved. He was not kidding, but he realized I was not ready for the truth.

Though my love for Rocco was still intense, I began to have trouble ignoring all the differences between us. This must be my fault, I told myself. I was convinced that love was enough to bind two people and overcome all dissimilarities. But my frustration was growing. Rocco seemed so little interested in the world and was content to live inside of a bar. I had so little understanding of love that I could not stand back and ask myself how this relationship was impacting me. I was becoming more focused on Rocco than on myself, which led to a sense of dissatisfaction that I was still unable to articulate.

I was living in a two-story home with two bedrooms. My next-door neighbor, who had AIDS, owned it. One day I noticed mouse droppings in the bottom kitchen cabinets. I set a trap. The following day, I caught a mouse, but more droppings appeared. I set out more traps, and more mice were caught. I then put out poison for the mice, as well as more traps. It seemed that there was no end to the procession of mice. As I lay on the sofa one evening watching TV, a mouse came out from under the sofa and seemed to be playing in the middle of the carpet, with no regard for me. This situation was too much.

The next plague to invade my living space was flies. I first noticed a larger than normal number of flies in the house after work one afternoon. I swatted them but more appeared. The next day I bought some bug spray, but the number of flies only increased. I kept my home clean, so I could not imagine where they were coming from. I kept all the windows closed, and yet, more flies. Parts of the house around the central heating unit were unfinished, and there were some open spaces in the walls in the kitchen area, so I closed those up with tape. Yet more flies.

I went to a hardware store and found some solid flying insect poison. I remember these orange strips hanging in our garage when I was a kid. Though toxic, I was desperate, and I thought I could hang them up for a few days while I was at work to get rid of all the flies.

The next day, before I went to work, I hung some poisonous fly strips, happy that I had the situation under control. When I returned eight hours later, underneath the fly strips, there was a black mass of hundreds of dead flies on the carpet. I looked under the other strip by the other window, and it was the same thing. I vacuumed them up. Then I noticed several flies flying around the living room. I decided to leave the strips up for another day. When I returned the next day, it was the same thing: a black mound of hundreds of flies underneath each strip and more flies flying around. I checked my food, underneath the sink, around the furnace, but could find no entry point. It was as if the biblical plagues were visiting me.

It got to the point that, after a week of this, I dreaded coming home after work because I didn't know what I would find: live mice or dead flies. My appeals to my landlord were met with silence, perhaps because his health was rapidly deteriorating and he was in the hospital. It was at that time that I decided that I had to move.

Part III: Hopes and Disappointments

Marion Barry was mayor of D.C., so there was an exodus from a bankrupt and out-of-control city. Housing prices were low, so I soon found a nice row house on Capitol Hill for a great price. I loved the property, but I wanted to consult with Rocco before going through with the purchase.

"Rocco, I may have found a house. Call me back. I want to talk with you about it," was my message. I did not receive a return call that afternoon. In the evening, I called again, left a message, but no return call. The next day I called once more, asking him to call me back, and said that it was urgent because I needed to make an offer on the house the following day and wanted his input. I never received a return call.

I went ahead with my offer and took the step of owning my first home. After twenty-four hours, the seller accepted my offer.

A few days later, I walked home from work in front of The Eagle and ducked in to get a paper and to see whether Rocco was there. It was so dark inside that it took a minute for my eyes to adjust, but I saw him sitting at the end of the bar, his usual place, with his drink. I grabbed the paper and left. He called out before the door shut, "Hey, hey, hey!!" and got up from his chair. I was angry because I wanted him to be involved in my decision to purchase a home. I listened to his side. "Mark, I have complete confidence in your ability to decide and choose, and I didn't want to get in the way of that. You know I love you and want the best for you, and I am behind anything you choose to do...." With these and other words, he gradually eroded my anger. Did I believe him? Not for a second. But I wanted to believe, and, at that moment, that was enough.

After being with Rocco for two years, the sex between us was almost non-existent. He would brag at the bar about us going at it all the time, but when we got home, he was always tired, and my desire for him had all but disappeared. I didn't have the experience yet to understand that the lack of sexual attraction stemmed from mounting resentments.

I bought the house and moved in; it was beautiful. To help with the mortgage payments, I got a roommate. That helped me financially but cut down on my privacy. This situation also affected my relationship with Rocco when he expressed discomfort in staying at my house with a stranger present.

Purchasing my own home gave me a sense of possession over my own life that I had not had before. I was tired of always going to the bar to see Rocco. At work, I spoke with him about this. "We hardly see each other outside of the bar!" I complained.

"We see each other at work every day," he said.

"That's not quality time. Can't we set aside, say one night a week, like a date night just for us?" He said he could not feel pinned down like that. I shook my head and let it drop.

Until this time, I had been going on the premise that love was enough to make a relationship work. I still loved Rocco, but so many things seemed missing, like a partially built house, but the materials to complete it were lacking. This feeling was confirmed on Valentine's Day.

I wanted to do something special for Rocco, so I decided to make a nice dinner. Dinner would be at seven o'clock; we agreed that morning. That evening I called Rocco at the bar (where I knew he would be after work) and told him the food would be half an hour late.

"That works for me! I need to relax for a while anyway." There was a slight slur in his voice. By 7:30, the food was done, but no Rocco. I waited until eight o'clock, then called again.

"Dinner is ready," I said cheerfully.

"I'll finish my drink and will be right there," he replied. Eight-thirty came and went, no Rocco. Nine o'clock, no Rocco. I became angry. I was hungry, the food was getting dry in the oven, it was Valentine's Day, and it was a work night. After ten o'clock, I decided to go ahead and eat because I hadn't eaten since lunchtime. Around 10:30, Rocco showed up at the door. I opened it.

"I'm here," he slurred.

"I already ate. Why are you so late? The dinner is ruined!" He looked at me and started to turn.

"Do you want me to go?"

I said, "No," and he came in. I fixed him a plate, and he ate his dinner on the sofa, watching TV, with me sitting next to him. This is not the way this is supposed to be, I thought to myself.

In retrospect, I realized that I did not end this increasingly dysfunctional relationship at this point because I still believed that my love for Rocco would somehow make up for his lack until he came around. This belief was more subtle than apparent, and I was unaware that my concept of love was emptying me of any sense of fulfillment. I was only ready to admit that I was running out of energy.

A week later, I said to Rocco, "I'm tired of doing all the work. Please take over maintaining our relationship for a while. You take the initiative to spend time together." Rocco agreed

"I'll take care of things, Mark, don't you worry."

Not long after this, Rocco told me that the leather/Levi club he belonged to at The Eagle was planning a New York trip, and I was welcome to come. I hadn't been to the city in years and looked forward to the trip and to the opportunity to bond again with Rocco. "Maybe we can go see the Statue of Liberty or the Metropolitan Art Museum," I suggested enthusiastically.

"Mark, I'm going with my club, and I'm going to be doing things with them. You're coming as a guest." My enthusiasm faded. "We won't have time to do that tourist stuff. It's like you're trying to take over the trip," he continued.

We both grew silent. I felt like a scolded child.

When the day of departure came, we met at Harry's house. A short, good-looking black man named Joseph was there whom Harry, Rocco's roommate, was dating at the time. Joseph was the driver. As we drove down the street, Joseph pulled out a six-pack, opened one, and guzzled the beer as he was driving. This was the first five minutes of the trip. I looked around at the others. I wanted to object. This was not acceptable. I did not feel safe with the driver drinking. But there was no reaction, no objection on their faces. I remembered Rocco's comment that I was a guest, so I kept my mouth shut.

We arrived safely at our destination. The plan was that we would share a suite and split the cost equally. When we got to our room, Harry and his companion quickly went into the private bedroom, leaving the sofa bed to Rocco and me. I objected. "We're all paying the same amount. It doesn't seem fair that they get the room, and we're out here." Rocco frowned and told me again that I just needed to go along with things. I was irritated. About an hour later, other club members arrived, and our room became the community center. Cigarettes were passed around, and soon the room was filled with smoke, burning my eyes, and making me cough. I left the room to take a walk. When I returned an hour later, the crowd was gone, Rocco was watching TV, and the room was still filled with smoke. I didn't say a word but proceeded to open all the windows to air it out. Rocco became irritated. "My eyes are burning," I explained.

"Mark, give it a rest," he said.

I felt like exploding, but I kept it in. Rocco planned to watch cartoons until we would all meet later at midnight at a bar called The Lure. I suggested that we go for a walk to break up the afternoon. He frowned. "Just for an hour, in our neighborhood," I suggested. He reluctantly agreed, so we left and walked down the street and looked in some shops; it was apparent that Rocco was not enjoying himself. I had my camera and asked a passerby to snap a shot of us. When I looked at this picture later, unhappiness was written on our faces.

There were many comments about what a hot couple we were; in fact, we were propositioned more than once at the bar that night. Men were circulating back and forth, up and down and around, looking to hook up. Rocco put his arm around me and said, "This one is all mine." His words rang hollow.

Rocco was not interested in sightseeing that next day, so he stayed in the hotel room while I wandered through the neighborhood. I returned to the room early in the afternoon, at which time we departed for home.

The trip had not renewed things between Rocco and me. It revealed even more that we had little or nothing in common. What had begun as an overwhelming loving feeling years before was becoming a sense of obligation filled with tension.

At this time, I decided to stop going to The Eagle to spend time with him. Rocco would need to make some effort.

Of course, Rocco took no initiative, so when I stopped going to the bar, I didn't see him at all, except at work.

Around Christmas time, my brother was going to get married in San Francisco, and I decided to return for the wedding. I hadn't been to California in several years, so I looked forward to the trip. The plan was to go to the wedding in San Francisco and then visit my sister in Los Angeles.

The months passed quickly, and the date of the wedding arrived.

I had forgotten how much I missed California as I rode into San Francisco from the airport. The skyline, the sunsets, the flowers, the climate; it was like paradise. It was good to see my family again. The wedding was somehow wonderful. I felt connected in a new and strange way. A few days later, I was at my sister's house in Los Angeles, sitting in the backyard under a banana tree, in 80-degree weather, in January! Could it get any better than this?

One evening, my sister and brother-in-law, both teachers, spoke with me about a career like theirs. I began to imagine myself in a classroom, making a real impact on people's lives while having a certain amount of creative freedom. The conversation planted a seed.

Part IV: What I Want in California

The seed turned into a desire that became a plan. The logical thing would be to teach in a school in D.C. or the surrounding area. I would need to enroll in college classes to complete the required courses. I soon discovered that the University of Washington, D.C. was in shambles. The Universities of Virginia and Maryland would charge me out-of-state fees, which were way beyond my means. I spoke with my sister about it. "If you teach in California, you could begin teaching immediately. You can take night classes to fulfill the requirements over time; because California is so desperate for instructors right now that the universities consider you to be a resident from the day you enroll." But this would mean a move out west.

I decided that I would continue my life as before but would merely investigate the possibility of entering California's teaching profession. The qualifying exam for teaching would be administered in New York City the following month. I signed up for it.

Two friends, Victor and Carl, offered to accompany me to New York. It would be interesting to experience New York again with these friends rather than with Rocco. I had to take the exam, and they wanted to enjoy the city, so we set out on our adventure. Carl had friends living in New York who offered to be our tour guides on our arrival Thursday night. "We'll meet you here at two o'clock," they said. In other words, for them (and for us) the evening out began at two o'clock in the morning! Because I didn't have to take the exam until Saturday, I agreed.

We bar hopped that night, going from one type of scene, or live show, to another. We finally ended up in a club with a stage where a bodybuilder/drag queen was performing. It was an African-American man with bulging, muscular arms and a thick neck who dressed and spoke like a woman. It was true that in New York, one can find everything.

The following day we all went our separate ways but then met for dinner to share our experiences. I was happy and was having fun.

The exam was easy, and soon we headed back to D.C. on a nice bus. We chatted enthusiastically about what we did, whom we met, and the next time we would make a trip together. As it grew silent on the bus, however, I began to reflect on these days. While in New York with Rocco, I was miserable, yet here I was happy. Why? I shared nothing in common with Rocco but a bygone feeling and a shared history. The love I had was not enough, and my once abundance of emotion and giving could no longer make up for his lack. I didn't know how to move on with my emotional life, however. So, I took the first step toward returning to California.

Once I received the test results, the next move would be to explore teaching positions out west. I would not have to accept if I were offered a job, I told myself. It was at this point that I spoke with Rocco.

"I'm not going to say anything to dissuade you, Mark. I want to encourage you to do what you think you should do." I almost wanted Rocco to object, to say one word to the tune of, "I'll miss you," or "I don't want you to go. What about us?" But there was none of that.

"The next step, then," I said, "is to go to California and set up some interviews just to see. Would you like to come with me?"

I was surprised when he said, "Yes."

We planned the trip for the spring and, as the months passed, I realized that I had no feelings for Rocco at all. I rarely saw him outside of work, but we were officially still a couple, and I still felt committed to him, on some level. It was as if our relationship had the structure of a building, with the beams and roof, but no walls, no rooms, no substance. But, somehow, it still stood.

That April, we first flew to San Francisco, where I had an interview set up in Oakland. Rocco enjoyed the city on his own the day I went to the meeting. I took BART to the district offices, waited, and waited, but the interviewer never showed up. After several hours, I wrote a note for the official I had an appointment with and left. When I contacted him later by phone, he was willing to hire me on the spot without ever meeting me. I took that as a sign that there was chaos in Oakland, so

I crossed it off my list.

Later that day, I found Rocco at one of the leather bars in San Francisco. He was sitting on a stool, sipping a drink, and seemed utterly content. He was a photocopy of who he was in D.C. when I first met him. I told him about my day. "Do you want to see the city tomorrow?" I asked. He agreed.

I was not out to my family at this point, and I thought I had everyone fooled; I claimed that Rocco was just my "friend." They knew the real deal, but I was not ready to come out because I was not entirely comfortable being gay.

When my brother offered to pick us up where we were staying, a gay Bed and Breakfast off Market Street, I was anxious that he would put two and two together. "We can just meet you somewhere," I said. "You don't have a car, and it's easier for me to come to your place," he replied. I acquiesced. When he showed up, I hoped he would not notice it was gay. It was simply my discomfort, not his, that I had not yet dealt with. So, we jumped into the car and drove up to Twin Peaks to see one of the most beautiful vistas in the world.

My brother did an excellent job showing the city to a newcomer, choosing the most impressive views and most characteristic buildings in San Francisco. However, we only had three days, and it was time to catch our flight to Los Angeles for the second set of interviews.

We stayed on the edge of West Hollywood at a motel in Beverly Hills, which sounded better than it was, but it was affordable. We had heard that West Hollywood was the hip, gay section of town but that the leather bars were in another area, Silver Lake. I wanted to see it all. "Do you want to explore a little?" I asked Rocco, who was lying on the bed watching cartoons.

"Sure," he said as he rose and put his boots on. A few minutes later, we were both walking down Santa Monica Boulevard, passing bars and restaurants. There was a younger crowd out, referred to as "Twinks" in the gay community. "Mark, I've seen enough," he said. Rocco felt out of his element; if it didn't resemble The Eagle, he did not feel comfortable; it was too far out in the world for him.

"Just a little bit more," I said. I wanted to walk down the whole Boulevard, see it all, and then return to the motel. I didn't see the point of being cooped up in a dingy room watching cartoons when there was a new city to explore. After a few more steps, he stopped.

"Mark, what are you doing? I want to go back!" he said, irritated. I turned because I was walking in front of him at this point.

"I want to continue. Why don't I just meet you back at the room?" I said.

"Fine," he said. We were angry at each other, but neither would own up. I was frustrated at his small-mindedness.

I kept walking to La Cienega Boulevard and was fascinated with the nightlife, everyone out on the streets; so different from Washington, D.C. Satisfied, I turned and made my way back. When I arrived at the motel room, Rocco was lying on the bed reading a comic book. I sat next to him. "Are you angry?" I asked.

"No, I'm fine," was his answer. I knew he wasn't fine but also knew that he didn't want to talk about it. "I'm going to go sit by the pool," he said and got up and left. I watched a bit of TV then went to bed.

Rocco came in much later and crawled in. I could feel the tension.

The following day I had an interview with a school official in Los Angeles. The interviewer described the entire bureaucratic process and said that I would have a better shot at landing a position if I applied to teach special education. "Would I have a guaranteed slot?" I asked.

"No. You could be offered a position in August," he replied.

"You mean I would move out here without knowing whether I had a job in the hope that I get offered one?" I said in disbelief. He nodded. That would not work for me.

My last interview was in East Los Angeles, in a small Hispanic community where my sister lived. It was a much more friendly experience than the others. They were impressed with my resume and asked me what I would want to teach. "My degree is in historical philosophy," I replied.

"Have you considered teaching world history? With your background, you would be a shoo-in. It is all about ancient Rome, the Middle Ages, and the Renaissance," the interviewer said.

"I would be open to that," I replied.

"Then we have a position for you. We would start you at this salary," and he gave me a figure which was much higher than what I was making. "Would you be interested?" he asked.

"Yes," I replied, without realizing the ramifications of this decision.

"Good. We will get the paperwork in place before you leave, and we will be all set. You just need to report on September third." We shook hands, and that was that. My life had taken a new turn.

When I arrived back at the motel, I told Rocco about the news, and I was happy. He said he was delighted for me. "I will try it for one year to see what it is like," I said—only having a one-year commitment to this lessened the impact of such a life-changing decision.

What I had come to California to accomplish was done. I had the job offer and a new future. I also had an ever-clearer revelation that Rocco and I were unhappy together. There was no common ground between us. So why did we stay together? At that point, I didn't know how to leave a relationship.

When we returned to D.C., the preparation phase would begin. Perhaps this step would resolve the emptiness that was growing in my heart.

Part V: Taking Back My Life

I had recently gotten a promotion at work, which I had applied for long before I planned the California trip. I had only been in the new position a month when I would have to give notice; this made me feel guilty, so I decided to speak with my immediate boss. He was a former priest who had made many changes in his life; he encouraged me to move forward with my life and to act in my own best interest, with no regrets. His phrase stuck in my mind: no regrets.

The most logical thing would be for me to remain in D.C. I just bought a house, I had a promotion at work, had friends, and had a relationship. I had never imagined that I would ever leave D.C. Even some of my friends thought it was a mistake. "Mark, this is crazy!" my friend Victor said one day. "You just got the house! Things at work are going well. Why would you want to risk all that?" he said.

"Because if I don't do this, I am afraid I will always regret it. If I don't try this now, it will be too late. Plus, I will teach for a year and rent out the house. If I leave my job on excellent terms, that door will remain open." It was a risk, but I was not afraid.

I didn't consider how this move would affect my relationship. Because I didn't know how to leave Rocco, or even if this was the right step, changing cities was easier than breaking up.

The months sped by, and the time of my departure approached. Marty, a friend of mine from California who was a former seminarian, flew out to accompany me on the road trip to Los Angeles. I couldn't wait to begin this adventure because I was focused ahead and avoided looking back.

It was not until the night before my departure that the emotional impact hit. I met Rocco at The Eagle, and we sat together, but I could say nothing. A mutual friend came up and began chatting. Rocco told him that I was leaving the next day. "Leaving for how long? Do you mean Mark is moving back to California? Leaving forever?" he asked in shock. At this, tears began to roll down my face. I was even surprised that I still had such an emotional connection to Rocco. This relationship had begun with such pain, yet promise. My mother had answered my prayers: I was together with the man of my dreams. But the promise faded as I realized Rocco was already married to The Eagle. So here I was, ready to leave it all behind. However, through my tears and sorrow, I did not doubt for one minute that this was the right step. No regrets, I whispered to myself.

That night I slept at Rocco's place; as we lay next to each other, he said, "I'm not going anywhere, Mark." It was one of the saddest nights of my life.

Rocco accompanied me back to my house the following day, where we met my traveling companion for the final packing. This only took about an hour as the dreaded moment of the final goodbye approached. When I looked at Rocco, I felt only love and compassion. Gone was the resentment and anger. "I love you," I told him as we hugged and kissed, holding each other. He did not manifest any emotion at all. I never knew how he really felt, if he felt anything, about my departure. As we pulled away, I looked out the rearview mirror and saw him standing in the middle of the street, waving.

My heart began to lift as we left the city, and my life in D.C. faded into the past as a new and unknown life opened.

Part VI: California Here I Come!

Ten days later, I arrived in Los Angeles; I soon found an apartment and was content with the beginnings of my new life. I still had some time before school began, so I joined a gym and set out to try to meet people. I soon became sexually active again and started to enjoy my freedom. The distance from Rocco felt good. I had a man in my life but could do what I wanted also. It seemed an ideal situation until I got a phone call from Rocco one evening. "You won't believe the news I got from work today!" he said excitedly. I waited. "They are sending me to work in the Lakewood office!" I was stunned and paused. "Aren't you happy?" he continued.

"That's great," I said with feigned enthusiasm.

Just as I was starting to enjoy my freedom here, Rocco would be returning to my daily life because Lakewood was forty-five minutes from Los Angeles. No, I did not feel happy about it. It wasn't that I wanted to break up with him; I just didn't want to see him for a while. The distance was doing me good. But he was coming, and I would have to deal with it.

My transfer to Los Angeles had not resolved the issues between Rocco and me. My feelings about his coming confirmed this. I was waiting for circumstances to change rather than changing them myself.

School started when Rocco arrived in September. Because he was lodged south of Los Angeles, we would see each other mostly on weekends. "Rocco, why don't I come down on Friday? I'm busy during the week doing lesson plans." He agreed.

When Friday arrived, I drove down to his extended stay hotel; we hugged and kissed. I still loved Rocco, but it had become a non-sexual relationship, and I still had no physical desire for him. "Why don't we go out for a bite?" he suggested. Over our meal, I shared my experiences as a new teacher, and he shared about his work in Lakewood. "It will probably only last a few months," he said. After our meal, he wanted to go out for a drink, so he drove us to a leather bar that looked, felt, and smelled very much like The Eagle.

"Hi Rocco," the bartender called out. Apparently, Rocco had been visiting this place nightly. He was exactly the same person he was in D.C., just transplanted out west.

Our lives continued in a parallel fashion, and we

saw each other on weekends only. "I'm tired tonight, Mark. Can we get together tomorrow?" he asked a few weeks later. At this point, we began to see each other only on Saturday evenings; I would sleep over, then Sunday afternoon return to my apartment. It felt more like an obligation than a desire.

When I was alone during the week, I sometimes thought back on the history of my relationship with Rocco and wondered why I had hung in there so long and why I was still with him. It dawned on me one day that I had a subtle but certain belief that Rocco would change. If I stuck it out, he would come around; he would start caring about me. With this belief, I waited. I always felt unsettled, and from early in the relationship, I would often ask Rocco how things were between us. "Mark, I have more experience than you in these things. I'm telling you, things are fine," he would say. Then a few months later, I would come up with the same question. I didn't feel things were fine, but I wanted them to be fine, so I clung to his words and tried to ignore my feelings.

Being focused on another more than on oneself can only lead to resentments, and soon I was where I was when I left D.C. Rocco found a new bar, and time together meant time there. Going to a movie or any other place was, again, like pulling teeth. But I put up with this because I was putting his feelings above my own.

When Rocco returned to D.C., I had some breathing space again. At this time, I met a man at the gym named Bradley, who was in a relationship, but who was open to friendship. I felt a physical attraction, but we saw each other only socially, and he began to tell me about the difficulties he was having in his disintegrating relationship. We started to see each other more frequently, and eventually, we broke the sexual barrier.

It was with Bradley that I experienced for the first time what it was like to be sought after by another man. This Bradley wanted to spend time with me whenever he was free. He would call me several times a day to check-in. This connection felt good. I was being pursued instead of being the pursuer.

As time passed, our friendship turned from being only sexual to emotional. As I had with Rocco, I found myself desiring that Bradley would leave his relationship to be with me. But I had some experience under my belt by this time, and I realized that, though I felt this way, it didn't mean I was supposed to be with Bradley. It became clear that he would not leave his relationship, and the new feelings for him were causing me pain. I decided to back away and take some space, which worked. It was like a medicine that drained much of the power of my system's attraction, and I told Bradley that I could not have sex with him anymore because it affected me emotionally. He brushed this aside as irrelevant and tried to seduce me anyway. I saw this as selfishness on his part, which made me back away even more and distance myself for my own good. This choice was one of the first times I had taken steps to take care of my heart.

But the experience with Bradley had left its mark. I felt more critical than ever of the dynamic between Rocco and me. My teaching career was going well. Returning to D.C. seemed absurd, and it was time to move forward with my life. I needed to leave Rocco for good.

48

Spring vacation was approaching, and I was having some trouble with managing my rental house in D.C. I decided to fly there over break to settle things. I also decided to end the relationship with Rocco once there. I did not know how to proceed, but I needed to anyway. I was resolved to return to Los Angeles free of this bond.

I felt that Rocco was losing interest, which was confirmed when I sent him my flight information. He said that he could not pick me up and asked me to take the Super Shuttle, and he would meet me at his house. I agreed to this, but it seemed strange that not having seen me in months, he couldn't be more accommodating. When I did arrive at his place, in his small room, I immediately sensed a distance. He didn't offer me dinner, nor did he have anything ready. I ate a sandwich in his kitchen and then, exhausted, fell asleep.

The next day Rocco had to go to work, so I was on my own and spent time with friends. But I knew I had to have "the talk" with him; the sooner, the better. I was nervous and scared, but some friends encouraged me. They had known about my relationship with Rocco for years and, from the beginning, thought it was a bad situation.

I waited until the evening to broach the subject. All my practiced lines faded. Rocco was lying next to me when I said, "Rocco, I'm not feeling right in our relationship." Before I even finished my phrase, he jumped out of bed and took up the subject.

"Mark, this isn't working for me at all. I mean, how long has it been since we've had sex? Also, I'm a top, and I never get any of that from you. Plus, you feel uncomfortable when I come on to you; I sense it. I don't know what is wrong with you, but this isn't working, and I want out!" I was stunned that he jumped at the opportunity to end our relationship. When I opened my mouth to give my side, he went into the bathroom. He was not interested in what I had to say. He came out later and turned out the light.

It became uncomfortable to be in the same room, much less the same bed, but it was late. "You're welcome to stay here the rest of your visit," he said. I lay there, under the covers, turned away from him, curled up, waiting until the morning light.

When Rocco got up to get ready for work, I pretended I was asleep because I was still at a loss at what to say. However, the minute he walked out, I sprung to my feet, packed my things, and got out of there. I had already alerted my friends, Victor and Barry, that I would need a place to stay, and they graciously offered their guest room. By 9 a.m. I was out the door.

I felt an overwhelming sense of liberation as I left that part of town and made my way to Dupont Circle. I was free of this weight on my heart, of the feeling that I needed to pretend to feel what I did not. But I was a little angered also. It was clear from Rocco's reaction that he had decided way before I had brought it up that he did not want to be in this relationship. How long ago had he decided? Months? Years?

When I was unpacked at my friends' house, I noticed that I had forgotten my glasses. I didn't have a key to get into Rocco's home, which would mean another awkward contact, but I needed the glasses. I left a message on his phone that I decided to stay with friends, and I said that I would appreciate it if he let me know how to get the glasses.

It was that evening that Rocco called Victor and said that he would drop my glasses off. Instead of ringing the doorbell, he called out from below, "Victor!" My friend went downstairs and returned a minute or two later, handing me the glasses. "I asked if he wanted to come up to say hello to you, but he said no, that he had a date." This also made me wonder how long Rocco had been dating others when we were supposedly together.

My friends congratulated me on the break, and I felt free and fulfilled. The rest of the visit went smoothly, and I returned to Los Angeles with some anger in my heart at Rocco but with a greater sense of possession over my own life.

Part VII: Lessons: One-Sided Love

One's first relationship is analogous to taking a prerequisite course. Mistakes are made, but invaluable life lessons can be learned.

Meeting Rocco was the beginning of a journey of self-acceptance and the abandonment of shame. Shame that I was gay and somehow felt less than a man. The shame of the need to love and be loved, which seemed like weakness. Shame of my willingness to love someone who didn't love me.

This shame diminished as the lessons learned hit home. Rocco was the first to show me that manhood and being gay was not a contradiction; masculinity and homosexuality can co-exist. This realization opened a way that I could live, grow, and flourish. My understanding of what it meant to be gay grew: not a being somehow trapped between two genders, as the color lavender is halfway between blue and pink. Some feel comfortable on that path. For myself, I wanted to embrace my masculinity and my homosexuality fully, and my relationship with Rocco was the beginning of that integration. Eventually, I would also meet others who could embrace both aspects of their person. I was grateful to Rocco for showing me this way.

With Rocco, I believed that love covered all differences, and though we had few common interests, I thought that love was enough to make the relationship work. As I showed interest in areas of his life, I thought he would eventually do the same. I felt that all I had to do was bring Rocco to museums, movies, and those cultural events that I enjoyed, and he would embrace them because he loved me. I didn't realize at the time that he had as little interest in these things as I had in sitting on a bar stool on a Saturday night. I eventually realized that it takes more than love to make a relationship work; love is like the mortar binding the house together, but bricks and glass and wood and pipes are also needed to construct that house.

I did not admire Rocco's life. His lack of relationship with his son showed neglect and abandonment. His living and work situation showed a lack of initiative. He had no drive to make his life different or better but was content to live in the same way for the next forty years. I ignored this, however. I loved him; he would change, he would come around, he would become that man that I loved, I repeated to myself subconsciously. But he didn't, and I matured out of this mindset.

Though love is the first necessary component of a healthy relationship, it is not the only one. If love is only a feeling, when this subsides, there is not much holding two people together, other than their shared history. Eventually, my feelings for Rocco did diminish, and it became clear to me what was clear to everyone we knew: that we had nothing in common and no genuine interest in each other. The relationship was a house built of cards.

The third lesson was difficult to admit but essential to move forward. I was willing to engage in a one-sided love with Rocco, ready to give myself to someone who was able to give so little. Because I had so little love in the past, I was willing to accept the crumb and put up with the neglect. But my heart knew what was best for me because eventually, this arrangement became unbearable. It took a stranger, Bradley, to show me what it felt like when someone sought me out, what it felt like when someone wanted to spend time together and wanted to communicate during the day. Once I realized how little I had been settling for, the relationship with Rocco was over, and I had to get out.

Perhaps my willingness to put up with such a one-sided situation stemmed from the fact that I had lost my mother to cancer as a child. That unconditional and embracing love had been absent as I matured into adulthood. So, I was willing to put myself on hold and wait for Rocco to change so that I might obtain a crumb of that love that I had longed for all my life. But it never came because I was looking for it in the wrong place.

As the years in this relationship passed, I waited for Rocco to become the loving partner I imagined. I waited and waited, but it never happened. As I left Washington D.C. and drove to my new life in California, I realized that if I could not accept someone exactly as he was, I had no business being with him.

Every relationship has its gift, whether a lasting bond or lessons learned. Through my relationship with Rocco, I realized that there is no contradiction between being fully a man and fully gay; I can embrace both and begin to feel comfortable with who I am. Falling in love with him also released the floodgates of suppressed emotions and love that I had kept under control for so long. Though I still didn't know how to deal with these feelings, their unleashing would become the energy that would help me grow and mature as I learned the ways of love. For this, I am grateful.

Chapter 2: Incomplete Love

Why love if losing hurts so much?
We love to know that we are not alone.
C.S. Lewis

Beliefs:

Moving in together does not equal commitment.

It is possible to back up to a previous stage in a relationship.

Avoiding talking about feelings saves one's partner from emotional injury.

Part I: The U-Haul Syndrome

I enjoyed being single for several months when I met Nathan, an African American, muscular man with strong masculinity yet a gentle voice. He was not a drinker; he was interested in spirituality, and, best of all, it required no effort to spend time together.

After our first meeting, we began to spend weekends together. I lived in Los Angeles, and he lived in Downey, but the commute was doable if we avoided Friday traffic. Nathan enjoyed doing simple things, such as going to movies and restaurants, riding bikes along the beach, and watching favorite TV shows together. His attitude was refreshing and felt right.

Unlike the previous relationship, I did not have an overwhelming falling-in-love experience with Nathan. It was a sexual relationship with affection and a growing bond, but it was not as intense. I wasn't sure, at this point, what it meant to fall in love because what I thought was love had led me to a very unhealthy relationship. Who is to say that this quieter and calmer feeling wasn't a more valid experience of falling in love than I had before?

I was going to the local university once a week to complete my teaching requirements. The campus was near Downey, so I began to stay with Nathan on Wednesday nights, commuting to work from his place; he stayed with me on weekends. I was becoming more attached to Nathan, though I wasn't sure that I was in love.

Nathan came from a deeply religious background, as did I, but his upbringing was more evangelical. This religiosity bound us in one way but also separated us because our religious traditions were so different. He struggled with reconciling his faith with his sexuality. Nathan was not out to his family, and he was pretty closeted all around. I didn't have any objection to that, but I could sense his suffering.

When the semester was over, I stopped going to Nathan's house during the week, and suddenly it felt like we did not see each other enough. I spoke with Nathan about this, and he felt the same. It was clear that our mutual affection was growing.

We continued this way for over a year when one day Nathan came to me with a proposition. "Mark, the house behind me is for rent. It has two bedrooms. We could share the rent and have a wonderful place."

Something about this didn't feel right.

"Isn't that just like getting married?" I asked.

Nathan responded, "It doesn't have to be that way. We could be just roommates who are dating. At least come and see it next weekend."

You sleep with your lover, not with your roommate, I thought to myself, but I brushed this concern aside. It couldn't hurt to look.

Over the week, I spoke with some friends about the possible move, and my friend Thomas said, "Well, if you move in together, the nature of your relationship will become crystal clear."

My commute to work would be the same, whether I lived in Los Angeles or Downey. My rent payment would also be the same. I could not think of any reason not to move in with Nathan, other than the sense that moving implied a more significant commitment. But Nathan had reassured me that this would not be the case, that we would be roommates dating, that things would remain very much as they were between us now. So, putting aside my reservations, I told Nathan, "Let's do it."

I gave notice to my landlord, and the following month Nathan came up with his truck to help me move. It was on that night that my misgivings that this was going too fast reached fever pitch. "You don't have to do this if you don't want to," Nathan said.

"No, we've come this far. I'll be OK," I reassured him. I did have doubts, but I felt it was too late to turn back.

Within the first week of living with Nathan, I knew the move was a mistake. It wasn't that we didn't care for each other, but whether we were willing to admit it or not, moving in together did constitute a commitment on a level that we had not yet reached. I was not aware of any communication issues when we were dating, but living under the same roof magnified the unseen problem. "I have to get up so much earlier than you, so I'll just sleep in my room tonight," Nathan suggested, and that is how we began sleeping apart, except on weekends. I thought that was what Nathan wanted, so I didn't raise objections.

I had not lived with someone before, and I soon discovered that rarely having any time by myself was challenging. When I lost my alone time, I felt irritated. Usually, I got home from work several hours before Nathan. When I arrived home one afternoon, about a month after the move, Nathan's car was parked out front. "Damn!" I muttered to myself, resigning myself to the fact that, after a day surrounded by students, I would have no alone time at all. I felt resentful, but I said nothing.

Still, life was not all bad. Nathan was a homebody, as I was, and we enjoyed the simple things together. But we had not learned how to communicate our feelings to each other, and I did not yet understand that this would become a critical obstacle to a lasting relationship.

About six months after my move, I went to San Francisco to visit family and friends for a long weekend while Nathan stayed behind. I had been faithful to him, though our sex life had been lagging lately. I was unsure why the sexual interest between us began to wane because we had not discussed it. Perhaps part of it was that we were sleeping in different rooms, and I came to prefer this. When Nathan and I slept together, he liked to cling to me, which often prevented me from sleeping. When I did doze off, he would change position and grab me from another angle, sometimes poking me with his hard penis. After a night of this, I always woke up exhausted from lack of sleep; Nathan was so sensitive that I said nothing because I didn't want to hurt his feelings.

On this trip to San Francisco, I spent time with family and a few friends. While staying in the Castro District, I met someone I was attracted to. We got a bite to eat and talked one afternoon. I did not tell him I had a boyfriend. After several hours, he asked if I wanted to see his house that he designed. "It's only a half-hour out. You will love it because it's on the beach. Come on by!" he implored. Finally, I accepted.

The house was incredible. As the sun set over the ocean, I found myself kissing him and, soon after, in his bed. He wanted me to spend the night, but I declined. "Give me your number; I want to see you again," he said.

"I work a lot, so that an email might be better," I said, bending the truth. Before I left, he told me he could fly down to Los Angeles the following weekend and every weekend after. I told him I wasn't ready for anything more. I was too ashamed to tell him I had someone already.

Afterward, this encounter made me feel terrible. By the following day, I lost the taste for San Francisco, so even though it was raining, I decided to return home early. I drove to Los Angeles in a storm. Instead of taking seven hours, it took thirteen to get there. When I finally got to the house, I was exhausted; it was a Saturday night. Nathan met me at the door and hugged me. He graciously threw together a sandwich. After I finished eating, I said to him, "Nathan, if you don't mind, I'm so exhausted I'm going to sleep by myself tonight. I'll sleep better."

Nathan's face fell. "We never get to be together," he said, dejected. He got up and went into his room, and closed the door. I felt bad and remained at the table, trying to figure out how to fix this. I felt bad about hurting his feelings; I felt terrible about being unfaithful. I felt bad all around, but most of all I felt tired, so I went into my bedroom, turned off the lights, and tried to forget it all.

Days turned into weeks, and Nathan seemed increasingly withdrawn. I knew he was upset; I knew it had to do with me, but I didn't know what the reason was. "Are you OK?" I would ask repeatedly.

"I'm fine. I'm just working stuff out in my head," he would respond.

Even though Downey was only 45 minutes from Los Angeles, I felt isolated. I had some friends in LA who were also my emotional support. I told Nathan that I would go up to LA every Tuesday to do errands and visit friends, which he seemed to understand. Though this gave me a sense of freedom on Tuesdays, my sense of isolation increased during the rest of the week. I began to feel sad, and my self-esteem began to sink. Nathan saw something in me that he didn't like but could not talk about. Our sex life all but stopped. We still only engaged in small talk.

On one of these Tuesdays, I was up in LA, and I went to work out at a gym in Hollywood. I met a handsome man in the locker room, and we chatted and flirted a bit but nothing more. On subsequent visits to the gym, we spoke again. There was a mutual interest. I did not tell him I had a boyfriend, but neither did I set up a date with him. But the whole thing didn't feel right.

Some weeks later, Nathan and I decided to come up to LA and go out to a bar where we would meet some of my friends visiting from out of town. The place was not too full when we arrived, so Nathan and I found a place to sit by the bar while our friends wandered. The music was pounding, the lighting was low, and the bar started to fill when it was past 11. "Hello Mark," I heard from behind me. When I turned, I recognized the man from the gym whom I had flirted with. "It's so great to see you here!" he said, obviously interested. Nathan turned, and I said, "This is Nathan," and they nodded to each other. I tried to make it evident that I was already with Nathan because he started to chat with me as if it were only he and I at the gym again. He eventually left. Nathan didn't say a word but was hurt. He was quiet for the rest of the evening, so I stopped having an enjoyable time.

Nathan would not talk about it when I asked him whether he was OK on our way home. The next day he did bring it up, however. "Here, you introduce me as Nathan. Not 'this is my boyfriend Nathan,' but just Nathan. That hurt me," he said.

I had no defense. I didn't want Nathan to know I had been flirting with this man. If I had introduced him as my boyfriend, I was afraid of a reaction such as "You never told me you had a boyfriend!" The whole thing was awkward, and I had caused this situation. I felt bad. My self-esteem sank further.

It became so apparent that Nathan and I had moved in together before establishing a commitment level with each other that would sustain us as a couple. We could not communicate about things that mattered, so small things were becoming huge problems. I was unhappy because I was tired of feeling bad most of the time. Nathan was unhappy also, though he did not admit it.

Part II: Readjusting the Coordinates

In three semesters, I completed my educational classes, so I was now free to teach at any school I desired. Reaching this milestone caused me to begin thinking that to improve things between Nathan and me, we needed to back up. If we returned to dating while living in separate residences, then maybe we could reach the point of making living together a success at some future time. I didn't speak with Nathan about this. I kept this to myself because I thought I would hurt his feelings once more.

"Nathan, I'm going to start floating my resume to see if I can get any response for the Fall semester," I told him one day.

"That's a clever idea," he said. I didn't mention that I would submit my resume up in Los Angeles.

My desire to move grew by the day as I began calling various schools for interviews. While this was going on, I sold my home in DC. The management of the property had become too complicated. The value had gone up, so I made about $50,000. I wanted to invest the money in a new property. Nathan and I started to look for a condo while I looked for a new job in LA.

My guilt about moving became the motivation for me to find a safe place for Nathan to live even though I was not yet sure I would get a new job or move back to Los Angeles.

I started going to interviews in Los Angeles when, after a few weeks of searching, Nathan and I found the perfect place in Downey: a two-bedroom, two-bath condo two blocks from a lake. Nathan had limited credit, so I paid the down payment and bought it in my name only. We had to do some cosmetic work, so we kept our rental for an extra month after escrow had closed. But the condo was ours, and the monthly payment was the same as what Nathan was paying when he lived alone.

I got several job offers during this time, and I accepted the one at a beautiful school in the western part of Los Angeles. The next step was to tell Nathan of my new job and that I needed to move closer to work. I dreaded this.

"Why don't you just try commuting for a while," Nathan pleaded with me when I broke the news.

"I already know it will be too far. Without traffic, it is 45 minutes; in traffic, it could be two hours!" was my reply. But the real reason was something else. I wanted to get away from a situation that made me sad; I wanted my own life back. But neither of us knew how to speak to the other about these essential things.

Until this relationship, I had understood communication as sharing the events of our lives. Telling the other what my day was like, sharing experiences, and communicating our points of view was sufficient until now. But when it came to feelings, I was at a loss. There was a growing misunderstanding between us and an increasing sense of responsibility for Nathan's feelings on my part, to the point that I felt unable to voice anything that I thought might hurt him. Yet, hurt Nathan, I did. We skirted around the essential questions, such as "Are you happy? Are you fulfilled? Are we growing together?" Talking about each another's day or the week's events became a way of avoiding the very things that concerned us the most.

With the job settled, I had to look for a place to live near the school. Nathan was paying the Downey condo mortgage, and I still had money left from the sale of the house in DC. Therefore, I contacted a real estate agent to see if there was affordable housing that I could purchase in the Los Angeles area. After several weeks of searching, I found a small but perfect one-bedroom condo in West Hollywood. I made an offer and soon had a new home.

It had been a year since I had moved to Downey, and I was eager to be back in more familiar territory and closer to my friends. When the day of moving came, Nathan was sad, which distressed me, but I was convinced I was doing the right thing. It was a feeling that became a conviction that I needed to live independently and that remaining with Nathan in Downey would mean my sinking deeper into sadness, depression, and feeling bad about myself. "We'll spend next weekend together, just like before," I said, as I kissed him goodbye. I could see the sadness in his eyes as he left. When I closed the door and looked around my place, I relished my space because I could close the door on sadness.

School began some weeks later as Nathan and I grew further apart, which felt right to me but not to him. We talked on the phone every night, sometimes during the day also. We planned our weekends together, sometimes staying with him in Downey or with me in West Hollywood. On one such weekend, he stayed with me on a Friday night. I got very little sleep because he was clinging to and poking me again. I was feeling particularly annoyed and exhausted the following day.

"Nathan, I enjoy being with you and sleeping with you," I began, "but when you hold me so tightly during the night, it wakes me up. Sometimes I get annoyed, but I don't want to be irritated with you. Can't we hug and cuddle together before we go to sleep, and then just hold hands as we doze off?" I asked. He looked downcast.

After a pause, he looked up and said, "But I want to hold you." We were at an impasse. I told him it made me uncomfortable, but he said he wanted to do it anyway. Again, I hurt him.

On weekends I liked to get back to West Hollywood on Sunday in the early afternoon, so I could prepare for the workweek and catch up on some of my things. This also pained Nathan. "We hardly have any time together at all," he said to me one Friday evening when I arrived.

"Can't we just enjoy the time we do have, instead of thinking about Sunday already?" I responded. But this didn't alleviate the shadow on his face.

It was some weeks later that the holidays brought the communication breakdown to culmination.

Christmas was approaching, and I planned the day with Nathan. He would come up the night before, and I would attend the midnight church service. Then we would make a lovely brunch the next day, open presents, and go to a movie in the afternoon.

I didn't know what to get Nathan for Christmas,

but I did know that the new condo he was living in needed lots of practical things. I remembered how my father had bought household gifts for my stepmother sometimes as a joke. He would buy her some pleasant things and wrap up a new broom or some other object needed for the house. I put together a big gourmet food basket, some homemade cookies, some glass flowers for his living room, and some other small gifts. Because he needed a fire extinguisher for the house, I also bought one and wrapped it up. This Christmas would become known as the Christmas of the fire extinguisher!

Nathan gave me one adorable gift: a guitar. He remembered that I had mentioned that I wanted to learn how to play. "I gave you lots of small things," I said, "eight or nine presents." He unwrapped the large food basket, the flowers, and other small gifts, which he seemed to like. "This is for the house," I said as I handed him the fire extinguisher. He unwrapped it and looked at me as if I were crazy. "What? You needed it!" I said, smiling. He shook his head and put it away. Later he told me that he understood that gift as a deliberate attempt to insult him.

It seemed that I could not avoid hurting Nathan's feelings. Things that I said or didn't say, do or didn't do, all impacted his heart and made him feel bad, and consequently, I felt terrible, too.

We planned a quiet New Years' Eve beginning in Downey. We would watch TV until 11, then drive to the beach, watch the fireworks, and wish each other a happy new year there. But Nathan was extremely withdrawn the whole evening. I didn't ask him whether he was OK because I knew it was some issue that he had with me, and I didn't want to hash it out. I didn't want to feel worse. We walked along the beach, and I tried to make conversation, but all his responses were brief. The feeling between us was so uncomfortable that I wanted midnight to arrive so the evening would be over.

"Happy new year, baby," I said and hugged and kissed him. He did the same; it was as if he was about to burst into tears. Again, I wasn't sure the exact reason for his sadness, but I was sure it was me.

We drove back to our condo in silence. I tried to make conversation, but it was pointless. I felt awkward. I crawled into bed next to Nathan and shut my eyes.

"You have to go this early?" Nathan asked, dejectedly, when I told him I was heading up after brunch.

"I need the day to get some work things done," I replied. This was not the reason but was a way to avoid being around his feelings. He was in pain, and this grieved me, so I fled. We hugged and kissed, then I got in my car and drove home.

Moving out had not improved things between Nathan and me. We could not back up and act like we were just dating again, build up to being boyfriends, then commit to each other, and eventually move back in together when we were ready. This is what I told myself would happen when I moved to West Hollywood. It was too late; history could not be undone. Nathan was becoming more despondent, and I was starting to dread the weekends together. But I continued to believe that this was just a slump that we would get through.

The belief that I could deconstruct a relationship and then build it up again was leaving out one key factor: two persons are not two buildings. The thoughts, feelings, and personalities of each one brought us to this painful point and could not be undone or ignored simply by a decision or a geographical move. If we failed to address the barriers between us and remained arrested in our abilities to communicate feelings and those things that mattered to each of us, we would eventually end up in the same place.

Part III: Looking to the Outside

A few weeks after New Year's, my friend Victor from DC came to visit. On a Saturday night, he asked if I wanted to go with him to a bar in Silver Lake. "Let me ask Nathan," I said, and Nathan accepted. The three of us went to the bar, entered, and ordered beers. Nathan and I stood by the wall watching as Victor wandered away to explore. But it was not a busy night, there was no excitement in the air, and both Nathan and I started to get bored after about an hour. When Victor returned, I said, "We're ready to go, but if you want to stay, you can. Just drop us off, and I'll give you the car."

Victor looked around and said, "No, there's nothin' here. Let's go." We walked out the front door as new patrons entered. When we were outside, Victor said excitedly, "Mark, I saw someone I think I know! He nodded to me. Can we just go in for a few minutes? Just for a little bit?"

I said, "Sure," so in we went, took our places along the wall, while Victor went to find the man he had recognized.

Nathan and I took a walk around the bar to the outside area. Because neither of us were drinkers or enjoyed just standing around, I glanced at my watch.

"Should we go see what Victor is up to?" I asked. With that, we went inside and saw him chatting with a very muscular man who was in his 50s. Nathan and I backed up and returned outside.

We gave Victor his time and space, and after a few minutes, he came outside. He said he had met this man, Warren, on another visit to California, and he wanted us to make his acquaintance before we left. We went inside and were introduced. I found Warren attractive because he had that stocky build that I was attracted to. After shaking hands, we left. Victor and Warren had made plans to get together the following day.

Nathan returned home, and Victor left early the following day to meet Warren to spend the day together. I saw Victor later that afternoon. He walked in with a grin. "Somebody had a fun time," I said. His grin widened.

"Mark, you gotta get to know Warren. You wouldn't believe his house, which is full of artwork. He likes history, and he's been all over. You would have a lot in common with him."

I nodded and then asked, "So what do you want to do today? I must shop for a new car. Want to come?" He accepted, and without another thought about Warren or the night before, we went to look at cars.

Victor returned to DC the following week but had left Warren's email address on my table. I was going to toss it out, but something prevented me, so there it sat.

At school, I was focusing on developing art history and weaving it into my world history classes. As I had always enjoyed art but had many holes in my knowledge, I began doing research. But I was facing some roadblocks in relating artistic currents to historical events.

One day I stood by my table and looked down at that email address. I thought, what the heck. I went to my computer and wrote Warren an email, introducing myself as Victor's friend from the bar. In that email, I shared my interest in art history and asked if I could pose him some questions. He responded almost immediately, and so our Internet contact began. I found myself looking forward to the online chats with Warren, which became a nightly occurrence.

Nathan complained, "Mark, sometimes when you say that you're going to bed, I see you are online."

"Well, sometimes I check my email and stuff before going to sleep," I replied. Nathan was upset, and I felt controlled. I didn't volunteer any more information.

"Why don't you come to visit me at my workshop?" Warren asked me during one chat session. I had not seen him in person since that night at the bar. I accepted. I planned a day when I was off work, so it would not interfere with my weekend with Nathan.

Warren ran an art restoration business, and his "shop" was a series of six garages in a small apartment complex he owned in the San Fernando Valley. I drove out there at about 11 a.m. and walked up the long driveway to where he was working. It was a warm day, and Warren had his shirt off, his hairy muscles glistening with sweat, as he cut and sized a frame. He apologized for the sweat and shook my hand. "I just need to finish up here, and then I'll take you to lunch." With one eye on his framing job and the other on his muscles, we chatted about art and his passion for restoring it.

At about noon, we left the shop and drove a short

distance to a nice restaurant with white walls and tablecloths. We sat in the garden area. Over lunch, Warren shared more of his life. "I have had a partner for 18 years, Timothy. He is only my second relationship. I was with my first partner Jim before that until he died of AIDs. Timothy and I have a difficult relationship. He doesn't work. He is an architect but mostly plays on the computer all day while I'm here," he said. We ended up speaking primarily about his tough time with Timothy while I told him little about Nathan.

"I've got to get back to work," Warren said after half an hour. "But let's do this again; this was fun," he said. I agreed.

I continued to chat with Warren online, and he proposed that I meet Timothy and he meets Nathan. "Why don't I give you a tour of the art museum in Pasadena," Warren suggested. We agreed, and I spoke with Nathan about these new friends, Warren and Timothy, and the idea of visiting the museum. Nathan agreed though he seemed uneasy about the whole thing.

As we drove to Warren's house in Pasadena a few weeks later, I could sense the unspoken resistance on Nathan's part. He didn't want to be here; he didn't want to go; he was doing this as a concession to me. I could hear it loud and clear, though he said nothing. He was irritable, but I didn't react. I wanted to have an enjoyable time at the museum, and I also hoped that the four of us could break the ice by spending time together.

When we arrived, Timothy let us in. Warren was working in the kitchen, again shirtless. I found him sexy, but I could sense Nathan was uneasy. "We'll wait for you in the living room," I said as we backed out. A few minutes later, he was dressed, and the four of us got in the car and drove down the hill to the museum a few miles away. "I did some of the framing and restoration work, so I know some of the pieces well," Warren explained. His partner Timothy smiled.

The art museum in Pasadena was larger than I expected, and its collection was of high quality. Warren acted as our tour guide and encouraged us to look at the pieces on our own, to pause in front of those works that drew us in. Warren sat down in front of a huge medieval painting of Christ ascending into heaven, surrounded by saints and angels. I sat next to him while Nathan remained behind. It was as if the spiritual world was bursting through that canvas. "I'm going to tell you something about me when we have some one-on-one time," I confided to him.

After two hours in the museum, we grew tired; we headed back to Warren's house. "Would you like to go to lunch?" Warren asked.

Without even looking at Nathan, I knew the answer. "I wish we could," I said, "but we have plans. But next time, sure." Nathan and I headed back to West Hollywood.

Things remained much the same between Nathan and me while I was feeling the pull toward Warren. Though I was physically attracted to Warren, there was no sign that it was mutual. But beyond this, his knowledge of art, history, and culture fascinated me, and I wanted to learn from him. I had never met anyone before who I was sexually attracted to and who shared my interests.

On Fridays, I stopped going down to Downey and

72

went Saturdays instead. I told Nathan that I was tired, but this also gave me a weekend evening to use as I pleased. On one of these Fridays, Warren and Timothy invited me to go to a movie, and I accepted. I called Nathan to ask him also. "I'm like an afterthought," he said, sadly, and declined. "You have the energy to go out with them, but not to come down to Downey," he continued.

"But I want you to come, too," I objected, but there was no convincing him. I decided to go out to the movies and have an enjoyable time, and Nathan could stay home and have a lousy evening if that's what he chose.

Looking outward instead of inward was a way of avoiding the discomfort of my relationship with Nathan. It was easier to make new friendships and find others who shared my interests rather than address what was causing the rift between Nathan and me. It was an avoidance that Nathan sensed since our time spent together felt increasingly forced.

Part IV: The Pain of Love

The sense of distance and sadness grew between Nathan and me, to the point that something had to be done. I loved him, but I was miserable when we were together. As the weekend approached, I found myself thinking of ways to minimize my time with him. I wasn't ready to give up on the relationship, but I began to believe that a temporary break would help. We could take a vacation from each other to see how this would make us feel. I told Nathan I wanted some space. "Whatever you want," is all he said. I could feel his pain once more, but I was so tired of feeling his pain. I knew I was hurting him, but I felt I could not continue living under this cloud. With that decision, my weekends were once more my own.

A few weeks later, Nathan called and asked whether I wanted to go to lunch that Saturday. He came up to West Hollywood, and we went to eat at a Western-themed tourist trap on Sunset Strip. We had a lovely meal and then headed back to my place. He was sad; I could feel it. We sat down on the sofa. "We aren't going to get back together again, are we?" he asked.

"I don't think so," I said, as tears began to run down my face. Nathan's eyes welled up also. He got up and left.

I had not wanted to admit to myself that my relationship with Nathan was ending. It was too harsh, too painful. I sent him an email. "Can I come to see you and spend some time in Downey next weekend?" He replied, "Yes."

I did go down to Downey the following weekend, and Nathan was in the condo that we had remodeled together. There was laundry piled everywhere, and the place was a mess. This was not like Nathan. "I've had a rough week," he explained. As I sat on the sofa and looked at him and looked at our place, I felt emotional. I excused myself and went to the bathroom. I closed the door and broke down. I regretted so much the pain I was causing him. I felt so sorry that things between us had reached this point.

I gathered up my feelings, wiped my eyes, and Nathan was still sitting on the sofa. I took his hand as tears welled up.

"I don't know what to say," Nathan said. I

apologized for the emotional outburst, thanked him for his time, then left.

Nathan and I would not see each other again.

Part V: Lessons: Not Ready

There had been a growing affection between Nathan and me, though there was never the powerful emotional experience I experienced with Rocco. But because my first relationship had been so dysfunctional, I supposed that the growing affection could be love.

When Nathan asked me to move in with him, self-doubt led me to accept. My gut told me that this amounted to a complete commitment. But my mind chose to ignore my gut. I could not think of any reason why I should not move in with Nathan, other than this discomfort at the base of my heart.

My gut had always been right. To ignore one's feelings always leads to those same emotions eventually rising and taking control at the most unexpected moment. One lesson of this relationship with Nathan was that it was necessary to listen to my heart, to what my feelings were communicating. They were often more perceptive than my mind.

Once Nathan and I moved in together, it became apparent that living under the same roof equaled a more significant commitment than we had realized. Suddenly finding ourselves accountable to the other for our whereabouts, our use of time, and about every other aspect of our daily lives came as a surprise. Being unprepared for this shift, I sometimes found myself resenting the loss of my autonomy. It was a move based on logistics rather than on a natural step within the relationship.

Our inability to communicate about things that truly mattered to us was barely noticeable when we were dating. We seemed compatible, shared some similarities in our backgrounds and interests, and had an excellent time together while dating. But the communication issue, once living together, became the umbrella that overshadowed all else and doomed the relationship from the first day I moved in.

To honestly know another person, one must be familiar with their thought process and emotional phases, and reactions. If one holds back on this emotional level, the other person is left guessing. Neither Nathan nor I had a clue on how to communicate honestly. I only knew that I was upsetting him some of the time and hurting him the rest, and because I cared for him, his hurt was too much for me to bear. But I could never just say this to him; instead, I came up with ways to distance myself. We were never able to bare ourselves entirely to each other.

Another belief that shaped my experience with Nathan was that we could undo history by backing up our relationship. After discovering that moving in together was premature, we could return to living separately and pick up where we left off when we were dating. We could then build up our relationship to the point of moving in together once we were both ready. This strategy seemed logical at the time. But there was so much pain and injury that had passed between Nathan and me. This pain, along with our communication barrier at a standstill, rendered this backtracking impossible. Nathan felt hurt, I was frustrated and sad, and changing the circumstances could not erase this.

A couple cannot "start over" if the causes of the initial difficulty are not addressed and resolved. But because I had little idea of how to communicate my feelings and did not want to hurt Nathan further, I held back. By not sharing what I truly felt and thought, I witnessed the very thing I had sought to preserve wilt, wither, and fade away.

Was my avoidance of talking about my feelings of sadness and frustration, as well as my doubts about our living situation and our relationship, saving Nathan from hurt and pain? This was my belief, but my experience proved it to be untrue. Rather than causing less pain, this holding back increased it. Why did I find it challenging to communicate to Nathan what I felt in my heart and burned in my mind and even he perceived? It was because I was trying to control his feelings by taking on an exaggerated sense of responsibility for his emotional state, which prevented me from opening my mouth and simply stating, "I feel this." I had no idea how Nathan would react, but I thought I did. Though we both were unable to reveal the deeper parts of ourselves, I had to take responsibility for the part I had played. I had to recognize that what another feels, or how he will react, is not under my control. Experience showed me that the belief that I could save someone from pain by hiding what I felt was not true, and this belief no longer served me.

Though painful for both of us, the relationship with Nathan brought a wealth of lessons. Through the growing affection between us, I realized that a feeling's intensity did not always manifest love. The importance of communicating feelings as well as thoughts, however uncomfortable, became clear through this relationship. The importance of basing the decision to move in together on a complete commitment rather than solving a logistical issue became a lesson that I could not forget. For this, I remain grateful.

Chapter 3: Love as Addiction

Immature love says: 'I love you because I need you.' Mature love says 'I need you because I love you.'
Erich Fromm

Beliefs:

> While dating someone already in a relationship, I can control my feelings.
> Loving someone is the same as loving his potential.
> Overcoming an addiction consists only in making a decision.
> Codependency: Rescuing equals love.

Part I: Dating a Married Man

I began to see Warren more frequently for lunch and discussions about art and history. On one of these occasions, I told him I wanted to share something very personal with him. "Warren, I used to be in a Catholic seminary. I studied in Rome for eight years and worked at a church for five years. Few people know this about me because I don't feel comfortable sharing it. But I wanted you to know…" I trailed off.

He smiled and said, "Mark, that is so cool! What an incredible experience that few people have had! Do you still go to church?" I replied in the affirmative.

"Can I go with you sometime?"

Warren and I had other discussions about my past in the church, and his positive reinforcement helped me grow. Before this time, my life seemed split into two parts: faith versus gay. I didn't see how they could be reconciled, so I hid my gay side from church friends, and I was paranoid that my gay friends would find out about my religious background. With Warren, the process of bridging these two areas began and my sense of shame dissipated. "You should write about your time in the seminary," he suggested one day. "I think it would be fascinating."

I had developed other friendships in Los Angeles, and one of these was Juan Luis, a man of Puerto Rican descent whom I met at the gym. He had a good heart but was burdened with many health problems, having contracted HIV through a blood transfusion while working in Africa. He had medical appointments every week, and sometimes he relied on his friends for transportation because he also had impaired vision. I told him about my friendship with Warren and introduced him to both Warren and his partner Timothy. One evening Juan Luis and I were invited to dinner at their house, and we had a pleasant evening until after the meal.

Warren liked to show guests his exquisite collection of Asian art, situated on the various levels of his four-story house. The lowest level was the bedroom, which was all jammed with art on the walls, tables, and bookshelves. Warren explained the objects while their small dog, Ginger, lay curled up on the bed. I became aware of a foul smell and looked around.

"Warren," I interrupted as I pointed down. Ginger

had pooped on the carpet, and we had all stepped on it, and we're tracking it around the room.

Warren turned to Timothy. "It's your job to clean that! Why didn't you?"

Timothy shrugged, and Warren continued, "I go to work every day and earn a living, and you are supposed to take care of the house" An argument was beginning. The odor was overpowering, and Juan Luis opened a window and leaned out. I backed off to give Warren and Timothy their space.

"Can't we do this another time?" Timothy asked. Warren agreed, and they cleaned up the mess together. We all went upstairs and thanked each other for the evening though their argument shook Juan Luis and me.

This incident showed that Warren's situation was complicated, and his relationship with his partner Timothy revealed anger and resentment. However, this didn't concern me because I didn't intend to get involved romantically with Warren. I was grateful that he was in a relationship because this created a natural boundary. I could be friends with Warren, but nothing more, and his relationship status supported my resolution.

Friendship felt safe, and we continued to share our common interests until one evening while chatting online, I revealed that I was feeling sexual. There was a pause, and he typed, "What are you going to do about that?"

Because my penis was doing the thinking rather than my head, I replied, "Why don't you come over?" There was a long pause.

"Are you sure?" he typed.

Before I allowed myself to think of the repercussions, I typed, "Yes." He responded that he could come over, but it would be late, past 10, and he could not stay the night. I told him I would see him at 10.

I was attracted to Warren initially, but I was now taking the step into a sexual relationship with no thought of how this might change things between us or affect our lives.

After 10, there was a knock at the door, and Warren stood there with two perfect white roses. He handed them to me, and I went to put them in a vase. Then he reached for my arm, and we faced each other. He almost lunged at me as we began to kiss. The kissing became more passionate and even aggressive until he reached for my shirt and ripped it off my body.

A minute later, I was against the wall with him pressing against me. Any uncertainty about whether Warren was physically attracted to me was put to rest as we began ripping each other's clothes off. I then took his hand and led him into the bedroom, where we devoured each other in passion for hours. It was a very intense sexual experience. "I'm sorry I have to leave," Warren said at about 1 in the morning. I was sad too, but he had Timothy at home, and I knew the limitations.

The next day at work, I could not get Warren out of my mind. I was utterly distracted and unfocused. When I called him during my lunch break and revealed this, he asked, "Is that a good or bad thing?"

"A good thing, because I want to see you again, and I'm feeling thrilled," was my reply. "Does Timothy know that you are coming over here?" I asked on one of these occasions. He didn't. "What explanation are you giving him?" Warren told Timothy that he was seeing a friend whom Timothy didn't know rather than telling him about me.

"Timothy might get jealous if he knows it is you, and then it will be more difficult for me to come over," he explained.

"Would you like to get together on the weekend, perhaps watch a movie?" he asked. I agreed, so our get-togethers became a weekly event, sometimes watching a movie or going out to eat, but always ending in sex.

Because I was in denial about dating a married man, I neglected to ask myself if this situation was good for me. Warren and I were seeing each other as friends, I told myself. His relationship, and how he dealt with that, was no concern of mine, I repeated. The choices Warren made revealed the man he was, and my own decisions were forming the person I was becoming. What I thought was a simple friendship soon became something outside of my control.

Part II: Chemical Love

As I got to know Warren better, I realized he was chemical friendly. I had never done drugs in my life and prided myself on that. I feared them and told myself that if I needed drugs to make myself happy, I needed to make some changes in other areas of my life to find happiness. But I came to discover that Warren was not only chemical friendly; he was chemically married.

This revelation occurred during one of our online chats. When he asked if he could bring drugs to my house, I didn't refuse; I was fearful and intrigued because this was a world I did not know.

"What do you use to get high?" I asked.

Warren replied, "I use Ketamine. It's an incredible hallucinogenic experience. If you want to try it with me sometime, let me know." I am still not sure, looking back now, why I didn't distance myself from Warren at that point. This was a red flag, a warning sign, a glaring red light saying, "Halt!" But I ignored it.

When Friday arrived, Warren was at my door with a gym bag. He pulled out little bottles and other supplies. He set to work preparing them.

He took a dose of Ketamine and, though he passed out, his legs were rigid, and his eyes were open. I waited by his side in bed, concerned that he wouldn't come to, but he eventually did. He was completely unaware that he was just on a drug trip and immediately reached for the drug again. Most of the night was spent watching him as he took the drug over and over. At a certain point, I had had enough and told him I needed to sleep. "You better not drive; can you sleep here?" I asked.

"Yes, I told Timothy I'm staying with a friend," he said. It took me about an hour to drift into an uneasy sleep as Warren was up and down all the time. At one point, I was wondering if he was still doing drugs in the bathroom, but I was too tired to check.

The next day, I was exhausted, but that night Warren was back again with his bag of tricks. I was taking my first steps into codependency.

Weeks went by. Every weekend Warren came over and got high. He would tell Timothy he was seeing a friend, and soon Timothy found someone to date also. Warren and Timothy were still together, but they both had boyfriends on the side. How I felt about this and where my choices were leading me were not questions that I was prepared to ask.

The world of codependency is analogous to a character in the Alice in Wonderland tale. Within that world, everything seems logical and in place. But if one looks in from the outside, everything is upside down and insane. I found myself drawn into the upside-down world of addiction and codependency without realizing it.

On Friday, Warren pulled into my garage, and another car pulled in quickly behind him. I was standing at the far end, holding the door open. Then suddenly, out of the vehicle behind Warren, Timothy jumped out. "I thought you said you were seeing a friend, but not Mark! You lied to me." An argument ensued.

About ten minutes later, Warren pushed the door open; Timothy had left. When we entered my condo, I asked him what had happened. "I'm glad it came out. I'm tired of the deception. He has always played around on the side; in fact, he is seeing someone now. So why can't I?" He seemed at peace with what had happened, though it had shaken me up. What role was I playing in these two men's lives, and how was this affecting their relationship and me?

I started to see a therapist and began to talk about my relationships with Nathan and Warren in my counseling sessions. I was looking for clarity, but in reality, I wanted someone to tell me that I was making the right choices. Instead, what the therapist said was, "Mark, look at these two people, Warren and Nathan. One is already in a relationship and is addicted to drugs. The other is single, sober, and still loves you. Why would you choose the former?" I resisted her comparison and wrote it off in my mind as black and white thinking. My feelings for Warren had gone too far, and I had lost my objectivity. It was as if my heart had utterly digested my mind.

I had believed that I could date Warren, who was already in a relationship and keep control over my feelings, but this belief turned out to be false. When he revealed his drug use rather than running, I became more enmeshed. I was making a choice to become romantically involved with a man who was married and who had a drug problem, and even when my therapist laid out the situation, I could not see it. My feelings were now obscuring my mind, and my emotional neediness was leading the charge. As I moved deeper into codependency, I lost sight of my ability to decide what was good for me and avoid what was harmful.

Part III: God and Addiction

My faith continued to be important, as I lived it in a quiet and personal way. Warren asked to accompany me to the Saturday evening services. Our routine, therefore, became Mass, followed by a night of getting high and then breakfast at the local shop.

At the church, Warren noticed an announcement in the bulletin; it was for a class offered to non-Catholics, or Catholics who wished to return to the practice of their faith. "Can I go to that?" he asked. I told him I would accompany him, so he began attending the weekly meetings at church to learn about the Catholic faith, at the end of which he could decide whether to convert to Catholicism. His background was Presbyterianism, which was not a stretch.

As our relationship continued to grow, I shared more with Warren about my years in a Roman seminary. "Why don't we plan a trip to Rome so you can show me your perspective on all the historical sites," he suggested. "But what about Timothy?" I asked.

"I'll handle Timothy. You plan the trip."

In the weeks that followed, I wondered what it would be like to go back to Rome again after leaving the seminary. Would a return visit make me feel guilty? Would it be consoling? Would it lift or break my spirit? It would be a return to my formal life that I had worked so hard to separate myself from. But this time, Warren would be with me. The planning began.

During this time, we started trolling the Internet, looking for other men to join us in threesomes. For every five hours spent on websites, we would perhaps snag one. So many hours were spent in front of the computer, instead of just with each other; the experience changed from looking in to looking out. We found men, some hot men, some not so much, some nice, some less nice, some who brought drugs, some who didn't. Looking for other men became an essential component of our time together.

I noticed changes in my body and became concerned. When I could not get over a sore throat and the doctor told me that I was suffering from exhaustion, I realized I needed to do something. "I need to get to bed before midnight on weekends." Warren agreed. I did not tell him not to bring drugs into my home because I felt a misplaced sense of responsibility. This is a symptom of codependency: to feel responsible for others but to neglect oneself. My reasoning at this time was that Warren would do drugs elsewhere or alone and put himself in danger. If he did them at my home, at least I could make sure he was safe. Warped reasoning, but I was deep inside of Wonderland and could not see from the outside.

But in the following weeks, his drug use did not diminish; it increased.

It was unusual for Warren to stay over during the week, but one night he asked if we could go out to dinner, then sleep together. I said, "Yes," but I needed to be asleep at ten because I had an important meeting the following day. He agreed, and we had a nice dinner, watched a bit of a movie, then turned the lights out and went to sleep. At about 2 in the morning, I heard a terrible crashing sound of glass breaking in my living room. I jumped up; Warren was not in bed. I rushed out to the living room to find that he was high on Ketamine and had fallen on my glass-topped coffee table. He was on a drug trip on the floor, with his eyes and mouth wide open, unaware of where he was or what had happened. Though he was so heavy, I managed to get him to the sofa and clean up the glass. After about 15 minutes, he began to regain consciousness. I explained what had happened, but his mind didn't seem to register the explanation. "Please, can we get to bed? I have to get up in a few hours," I pleaded. I helped him to the bed, but I was so shaken that I didn't sleep the rest of the night. I drove to the school exhausted and was not pleased with how my meeting went.

I finally began to form the word in my mind: "ADDICTION."

Why did I stay in a relationship with Warren? I believed that his drug use was a phase that he would soon pass through. The day would arrive when he would decide to give up substance use, and then our lives would stabilize, I thought. Having no previous experience with addicts, I felt that Warren simply had to wake up one day and decide that he had had enough; he would then live a drug-free life. Support systems, rehab, 12 step programs were all foreign to me.

I also failed to grasp the contradictions in the choices that Warren and I were making. What did faith have to do with the direction my life was taking? Was this why I was brought to this point by all the rich experiences of my life? Was I placed on this earth to care for a man using drugs? Was this my lot? These questions were under the surface but could not remain there forever.

Part IV: Rome: Some Things Change, Others Remain

I looked forward to the trip to Rome because it would add a different focus to our relationship. I could share more of my history with Warren and re-experience Rome so many years after leaving the seminary. I looked forward to the trip yet felt uneasy. Rome was so familiar, so much part of my story. What memories would it stir? Would I be happy looking back or sad?

We had booked a hotel near the Roman Forum, around the corner from the Angelicum, where I had done my undergraduate studies. As the plane touched down, and later as we approached the hotel in a taxi, I had a feeling of coming home. Rome felt like the embrace of a mother. There was something safe, yet magical, about the city. To experience Rome is like developing a relationship with someone who gets into your mind and heart and veins and becomes part of who you are. Rome is like falling in love with a woman who, if you remain far away too long, draws you back into her arms through a subtle longing in your dreams, your thoughts, your very being.

Warren had been to this city many times and had seen all the main sights, but I promised him I would show him Rome underground. We shared an interest in archeology, so I arranged a tour underneath St. Peter's, all the way to the tomb of the Apostle. Over the following days, we continued our exploration of underground Rome at the catacombs and then on an archeological tour of the Palatine hill.

Warren was so happy over dinner one night. "You have shown me that there is always something new to see in Rome, and now I get to see it through your eyes!" he said.

"I've never seen you smile this much," I responded.

"I can say the same about you!" and he was right.

This was the happiest I would ever see Warren.

A few days later, we walked up to the Janiculum Hill, past the North American College where I spent three years in the seminary. We continued walking until we reached a level from which we could see the whole city below. Warren stood beside me as I looked in the distance and could see the Vatican, where I would go to pray, and on the other side, Piazza Navona, where I used to meet my friends in the evenings, and further out the Pyramid, from where I would catch the train to the beach at Ostia. I could see my whole life in brick and marble and train tracks. "Mark," Warren said, interrupting my thoughts. "How does all this make you feel?"

I paused. "It makes me feel...happy." We stood

there quietly for a while and then headed back down the hill.

Notwithstanding the problems, I loved Warren. I still believed that the drugs would become a distant memory.

The days passed quickly, and we decided to spend our last night in a better hotel near the Vatican. The room was huge by Roman standards, exceptionally clean, and we were both happy with it. We spent a day close to the heartbeat of the Catholic Church. I went down to the chapel near the tomb of St. Peter to pray; we paused in front of La Pieta; we went to a religious goods store and then spent time at St. Anne's church inside the Vatican walls.

That night Warren called Timothy to check in on him and discovered that there was trouble at home. Timothy also had a taste for Ketamine and had been getting high alone when he fell and broke a window. He called 911, and an ambulance came, as well as the police. He was not injured seriously because they did not take him to the hospital, but the police found Warren's drug stash and confiscated it.

Warren and Timothy started to argue long distance. First, Warren hung upon him. Timothy called back, and then he hung up on Warren. Warren turned to me for support, but I didn't want to get involved. The two went back and forth, calling each other and hanging up on each other repeatedly. "Aren't you going to say something?" he asked me angrily.

I shook my head.

"You're either with me, or you're on his side!" he said, but I still kept silent. After the two of them had finished their argument, Warren stomped out of the room. "I'm going to St. Peters," he said. It was about nine o'clock at night.

When he returned later, he complained that the gates were closed, and it seemed to him that not even God cared about what he was going through. I wasn't sure what to do or what to say because I knew better. "Is he OK?" I asked.

"He's fine! He's a child!"

After a pause, I said, "Well, I'm sorry this happened, and I'm sorry that you have to go through this now, the last night in Rome." Then I lay down to sleep.

I clung to a belief that caused me to remain in this relationship: I thought I could be in love with a man's potential. Not loving the man he was, but love the man he could be. This led me to excuse unacceptable behaviors as I looked at some future unknown date when Warren would mature into that man I had so clearly pictured in my mind. But this was not real because this man existed only in my imagination.

Part V: Choices and Sacrifices

When we returned home, Warren became busy with his art business and his Timothy situation. I was still on my summer break, so I spent time with my closest friends, Thomas and Juan Luis. The three of us got together for dinners several times that week that I returned.

Juan Luis had been cultivating a friendship with Timothy over the past months, and they sometimes met for a meal, or Juan Luis asked Timothy to drive him to a doctor's appointment.

One evening Juan Luis was having a get-together

at his place. He confided to Timothy that he felt uncomfortable inviting Warren and me because we were together in some type of undefined relationship. Juan Luis didn't want to have any part of it. I only heard about this from Warren, who called me as I was driving home from work. "Did you hear what that fucking Juan Luis said? How dare he judge me! Does he think he's better than anyone else? I will not ever speak to him again. You're going to have to choose between him and me. I can't be around you if you keep such company!" He continued in this way for some time, venting his anger at feeling judged by Juan Luis.

I felt caught between a relationship and a friendship. At that point in my life, wanting to avoid stress, I decided to back away from Juan Luis until this blew over. When things settled down with Warren, I thought to myself; I would renew my friendship with Juan Luis and pick up where we left off. I didn't yet have the perspective to realize how unhealthy a choice that was.

Romantic love versus friendship love had never conflicted with me. But I was so desirous of romantic love that I was willing to pay a hefty price.

Early on in our relationship, Warren had expressed a desire to invest in a piece of property together. The thought appealed to me emotionally because it meant a lasting, though undefined, relationship. I was still in love with Warren's potential and was convinced that his outstanding qualities would eclipse negative ones once his drug use and unhealthy relationship with Timothy were behind him. Blinded to the present, I believed in an ideal future.

"Mark, you shouldn't buy a property with someone who is not your partner," a friend of mine advised me, but my ears could not hear it.

As the discussions about purchasing a house continued, I approached Warren about his drug use. It was time to put it in the past.

"I'm not ready to make that choice," was his reply.

"That is your choice, but just be sure you can accept the consequences." He said nothing.

As we began to look at properties, I pushed other concerns aside. Finding the right place became our focus.

We found a home in an area just outside of Los Angeles, a community called Mt. Washington, which in its lowlands was gang city, but had hills with lovely homes and splendid views. It was a two-bedroom, one bath with a massive piece of land, four lots. Warren fell in love with it immediately.

When we spoke of the property that evening, I told Warren that this was not the house I wanted to buy. At this, he grew furious, accusing me of playing games and of having no intention of investing with him. I was surprised at these accusations, tried to explain my reasoning but then let the matter drop.

Warren's emotional attack had unsettled me. In the days that followed, he never said he was sorry nor mentioned the matter again. He immediately resumed being the sweet and considerate man I had known at the beginning. My hurt feelings eventually dissipated without being addressed, and I soon began looking at properties again.

It was during this house search that I received a disturbing phone call from my friend Bradley. "Mark, did you hear the news? Juan Luis passed away! He was in the hospital for a few days, and his organs began to fail, and he is gone." I hung up the phone. I never had the chance to reconcile with the friend I had pushed aside. I had sacrificed a friendship to preserve a romantic relationship.

Loving someone's potential is a denial mechanism employed once one's sense of well-being is placed in another rather than oneself. I had no evidence to support that Warren would either give up drugs or stop being abusive when there was a disagreement. Yet, the growing sense of codependency convinced me that Warren was essential to my happiness and that he needed me. Life would have to show me whether these convictions would hold.

Part VI: I Want to Believe

The prospect of investing in property together gave me a new clarity of what I could tolerate, so I had a conversation with Warren to lay down my conditions. "I cannot buy a house with you if you are still doing drugs," I said. "It is too risky for me. If you decide you can stop, we can move forward. If not, we need to wait."

Warren agreed. "I will not do drugs anymore, I promise." I believed him.

As we searched for properties on the Multiple Listing Service, I saw a photo and a description of a probate triplex on a hill overlooking Hollywood. I liked what I saw and decided to drive out to it the next day. It was on a winding street, with balconies on two stories and a red, blooming bougainvillea vine crawling up the side. I walked up the stairs to get a better look, and when I turned, I looked down at the view. I could see the Hollywood sign on the right, Century City in the distance, and the ocean to the left. I peered inside the window; it was dark inside, but I could see the panorama through the living room window. My heart was beating fast. I called Warren immediately.

Warren had planned a trip and was scheduled to leave town the next day. "I can see it when I get back," he said when he returned my call.

"I don't think this place will be on the market when you return," I said. He made arrangements with the realtor, and we got to the property that night.

When we entered the second-floor unit, the first thing that struck the three of us was the smell; it was the odor of rotting food or something decomposing. "The owner died, and the house has been in probate for twelve months, with no one living there. But there are tenants, one in the unit above and one below," the realtor explained. We stepped in and noticed that there was an orange 1970s era shag carpet that was so dirty that, in some places, it was black. The walls were very dark, with 1970s faux wood paneling. But the view drew us toward the large picture window that looked out at the shining city below. The place needed to be renovated, but the view itself was worth the asking price. "I like it," Warren said.

"I love it," I said. We both turned to our realtor. "Let's make an offer." The process of purchasing a property together began.

Warren and I continued to spend weekends together without drugs. I felt relieved. However, when he stayed over, I noticed that he was up and down all night long, never being able to get a good night's sleep. I wondered about this and began to suspect that something was going on.

On one such night, I awoke and lay there a long time; Warren was not in bed. I listened closely and heard faint sounds in the kitchen. I could hear one of the burners on the stove ignited. I got out of bed ever so quietly, tiptoed to the kitchen, and turned the corner. At that instant, Warren saw me. He had a pipe filled with Crystal Meth in his hand. He threw it behind the microwave, turned off the stove, and stared. My mouth fell open. "You're doing Crystal? You promised you wouldn't. What the hell is going on?" He said nothing. Shocked, I fled the scene, down the street, until I sat on someone's doorstep for several hours to think.

By the time I had returned, I was calm. I had made some decisions. "Warren, come sit down," I said. "The three things that will cause me to leave a relationship are drug addiction, physical abuse, and emotional abuse. Therefore, I will not go through with the purchase of the house if you are still doing drugs. We can use the inspection results as grounds to pull out of the deal. I don't know where your mind is on this; you must tell me so I can know what direction to take here. You can think about it and let me know tomorrow, but you need to decide." At that time, I still believed that one had only to decide to give up the substance, which would fix it.

"Mark, I promise I will never do Crystal or other drugs again. While you were out, I dumped all the Crystal down the toilet. I want to get this house with you more than anything else. I am so sorry for tonight, and I promise it will never happen again."

I chose to believe his words and to move forward with the purchase of the triplex. I did not yet understand that the best predictor of future actions is past behavior patterns, and I put much weight on Warren's promise because I wanted to believe his words were true.

With the building's purchase completed, the renovation work began, and the tension between us rose. Whether it was decisions about paint colors or simply our daily interactions, it seemed I could not say, or do, anything without provoking Warren's anger. I felt a growing mountain of resentment on his part, and I suggested that we go to couples counseling to work these things through. He agreed.

During the first session, Warren burst out, "I'm angry! I guess I'm just an angry man. That's what you think, huh? You think you're better than me! Stopping the drugs was not a joint decision. You just dictated your decision to me!"

He continued in this way until I interjected, "I gave you a choice. If you wanted to continue using, I would have looked for a new house on my own…"

Warren interrupted me. "You're a dictator! You need to control it all, don't you? You had no right to make that decision."

Finally, the counselor broke this up and managed to calm Warren down. "We'll deal with this over several sessions," he suggested as a conclusion. "In the meantime, I would suggest that both of you think about what belongs to you, and what belongs to the other person, and where that boundary lies."

As we drove home, Warren was even more furious at me than before, so I kept my mouth shut and let him vent. Was this love?

One morning I was doing laundry, and I found a vial in Warren's pocket. It had tiny crystals in it, and I asked him what it was. "It's for an art project," he said, but I recognized Crystal Meth when I saw it.

The signs were in front of me that Warren was still in the grip of drugs. Mood swings, angry outbursts, and unpredictable behavior. But now we owned a home together; we were bound. I had sunk my roots deep into this still undefined relationship and could not easily back out. I withdrew more until something occurred which neither of us could deny nor ignore.

Part VII: Powerlessness over Another

One night Warren had an ache in his side and a low fever. I felt his forehead. I shook my head. "Please take really good care of yourself," I pleaded. At this, Warren rose in anger. "What the hell are you implying? You think this is drugs, too! You think you know it all! You're so fucking judgmental all the time!" I remained silent.

The next day Warren got worse. He was lying in bed, moaning from the pain. I put my hand on the area and prayed. When the fever went up the following evening, the pain was even more intense; I convinced Warren to let me bring him to the emergency room. I called Timothy and asked him to meet us there.

Warren was put into a bed, tests were run, but the doctors were baffled.

"We'll just have to wait until whatever it is manifests itself," the doctor said. At this, Warren started to get up, thinking that he could go home.

"No, Warren, you have to stay," Timothy said. Warren was very weak and ill. His eyes welled up when he realized he could not leave.

"Mark, I'll stay. Why don't you go home and get some sleep," Timothy suggested. I agreed and returned to the half-completed house.

I worked during the day and could only come after classes to see Warren in the hospital; each day that passed, I grew more frustrated and fearful. Lacking a diagnosis, the doctors only had him on morphine. They were not treating whatever the cause was. A week had passed, and Warren seemed to be getting worse.

I feared losing Warren. Though we had our difficulties, I still hoped for a bright, loving, and stable future with him. I prayed, hoped, and worried.

One day a new doctor appeared on the scene, Dr. Chow, who sat down and spent some time with Warren. "Can I ask you some personal questions in front of them?" he asked, referring to me and another friend of Warren's, Jay, who happened to be present. Warren nodded. After asking him about his symptoms, Dr. Chow got closer to Warren and asked in a faint voice, "Are you an intravenous drug user?"

Warren said, "Yes."

"OK," Dr. Chow replied. "I may be on to something," and he left. I followed him out of the room as he went to a computer monitor.

"What do you think it might be, doctor?" I asked. He replied, "I'm not sure, but it sounds like an infection in his heart caused by intravenous drug use, perhaps a dirty needle. I'm going to have some tests run, and by tomorrow we will know for sure." He ordered the tests, blood was drawn, and we all waited.

Though I was devastated by the news of his intravenous drug use, I was relieved when the test results showed that Dr. Chow was correct because we now had a diagnosis that could be treated. They immediately started administering the most potent antibiotics they had, and after a few days, Warren seemed to be getting better.

It was during this time that I began to question whether I wanted to stay with Warren. He had broken his promise about the drugs. What kind of a future would this be, I wondered. But I couldn't make this decision now, I thought. The priority was to get Warren well, so I pushed these thoughts aside.

I began to go to Al-Anon meetings because I did not know how to cope. The message I kept hearing was, "keep the focus on yourself because you cannot change another." At that first meeting, I spoke up and said, "I feel like I'm in a dark room, and I keep bumping into things. I'm here because I need some sort of a map to lead me out of this." Some people chuckled. But I kept going back.

It was going on a month that Warren was in the hospital; he was doing better now, though very weak. There was even talk of him coming home, but then the fever returned. His doctor asked to have a conversation with Warren and asked me to be present.

"We may have to do something more drastic here. Using antibiotics is like throwing mold at the infection, and yours may be too far along. I'm going to bring in some other physicians because I think we may need to go in and surgically remove the infection. Anything remaining after that will be taken care of by the antibiotics."

I broke in, "Is this the worst-case scenario, then?"

He said, "No. The worst-case scenario would be for the infection to advance and for us to do nothing. With surgery, we can remove it, and once we are in there, we can see if there is any damage to the heart. But I anticipate a full recovery, though your quality of life will be different from before." I wondered at his words.

"What could be affected by the surgery?"

He paused and then replied, "Well, with any surgery, there is a chance of losing the patient, though I don't anticipate that. Besides that, we will have to see what we find when we go in."

The surgeons got involved, the diagnosis was made, and the surgery was decided. They would go in from the side to reach the area of the heart and remove the puss. They anticipated having to remove some of the vertebrae, cleansing them from the infection, and replacing them like a puzzle. Warren could experience chronic back pain after the surgery, but this was hard to anticipate. The doctors decided that this was the best solution.

As we prepared for the surgery and its aftermath, all the past months' stress and worry started to take their toll. I was feeling overwhelmed and exhausted. I devised a plan to motivate myself. After Warren was home and sufficiently recovered, I would reward myself with a trip to Rome.

Rome was a consoling and healing city for me. When I traveled there last time, I felt changed; some type of growth seemed to happen in some unexpected area of my life. Because I had friends living there, I could stay with them. It was decided, I told myself. I would go to Rome. But I said nothing to Warren.

The day before the surgery, I visited Warren with a longtime friend of his, Kerry. As we entered, even Kerry was shocked at how Warren looked. His skin had a grey tone, he was weak, and when we walked in, he was crying because the pain was so great. I held his hand, and Kerry stood above him, trying to lighten the mood by cracking jokes. Kerry was hyperactive and could not stay in one place very long, so after about thirty minutes, we left, and I promised Warren I would return that evening, alone, which I did.

When I returned that night, Warren was sad. "Honey, sit here next to me," he said, so I sat on the bed, and he took my hand. "I may not make it through the surgery," he began. I shook my head, but he continued, "If I don't, will you take Ginger (his little dog) for me? Timothy will neglect her. And can you also return all the clients' artwork for me? It is all labeled and in the garages. The house will be yours; I put enough money in the joint house fund to complete it. I want to tell you, Mark, that I love you so much..." He broke off and began to cry. "I love you so much, and you have made me so happy since we met. I'm so sorry for the pain and suffering I have caused you. I never meant to cause you any pain. I'm so sorry about the drugs." He began to cry again and sob. I took him in my arms and reassured him that everything would be OK. I wasn't sure myself at this point, and I was scared.

The following day Warren was already being prepped for surgery when I arrived at the hospital, so I didn't get to see him. After going stir crazy in the waiting room for two hours, I decided to leave the hospital to do an errand.

Just as I was pulling into a store parking lot, I got a call from the surgeon. "Is this Mark? Mark, I wanted to tell you that Warren is out of surgery already, and everything went fine. You can see him once he is out of recovery in about two hours." I was so grateful and thanked God for answering my prayers.

Kerry asked to accompany me to see Warren. As we entered the recovery room, I saw the change immediately. Warren's face was now pink instead of grey, he was sitting up instead of flat on his back as he had been for weeks, and he had his legs crossed, something that he only did when he was comfortable. Even though he was hooked up to several machines, he looked so much better than the day before.

Warren told us, "The surgeon said he was surprised at how much puss there was, the size of a baseball. It had a film that had formed around it, and that's why the antibiotics couldn't penetrate. He had to come in from the side and go around my lung to get at the infection. They also had to rebuild some of my vertebrae," he said, showing us the bandage. Kerry became excited and started asking Warren many questions, telling him stories, and making jokes a hundred miles per hour. This was Kerry's way. After about fifteen minutes, Warren said, "This is all too much for me, and I need to rest. I'll see you later," and with that, we left.

Warren's recovery began to move forward at lightning speed. The following week, he asked, "Mark, can I come to stay with you once I am released?" Because he was still living at his house in Pasadena with Timothy, this was a new step. This was how the decision to live together was made.

Timothy didn't like the idea and repeatedly told Warren that he belonged in Pasadena. They went around in circles about this, but I kept out of it.

The house was nearly complete when I picked Warren up from the hospital the following week and drove him home. He marveled at the trees, the flowers, the stores, the people on the sidewalks; it had been two months that he had been in the hospital. He had trouble walking, so I helped him up the stairs and then onto the bed. I set to work immediately to make his meals because his weight loss had been significant. Caretaking came naturally to me. The next day a physical therapist would come to get him walking on his own again. I was off for the next few months due to school vacation, so I would have the time to take care of Warren full time.

When I spoke with my best friend, Thomas, about the whole sickness and hospitalization, he said, "Well, the good thing is that Warren's drug-using days are behind him, and this was his bottom. Now hopefully, you can move on with your lives." I was happy that something positive could come from this tragedy.

Since my childhood, I equated caretaking with love. Having a mother who battled cancer for years, putting another's needs before my own came as second nature. When Warren was fighting for his health in the hospital, caring for him was the same thing as loving and being committed to him, I believed. But this arrangement left me feeling confused, empty, and unhappy. To focus on me seemed selfish, especially because Warren's need was so great. Though I devoted myself entirely to Warren's recovery, I began to wonder where I had lost myself along the way. Warren's addiction and health problems overshadowed and diminished the importance of giving to anything I needed or wanted. But this seemed to be the life I was destined to live. I felt that I had no choices.

Part VIII: From Hope to Disappointment

For two months, I took care of Warren, making him three large meals a day, helping with his physical therapy, changing his bandages, and taking him back and forth to doctor appointments. Ginger, his faithful little dog, a mix between an Italian greyhound and a Jack Russell (a Jack Russell on stilts), was always at his side. She seemed so grateful to have him home.

"The doctor says I'll never be the same," Warren would complain. I encouraged him to look on the bright side, but I didn't know how he would ultimately heal because part of his vertebrae had been rebuilt, and the doctors hoped it would heal and repair itself. The drugs had taken their toll. The once muscular bodybuilder who never even got a cold now looked feeble. He needed to sleep a lot, got winded easily, and had trouble walking up the stairs. It broke my heart.

When it was time for me to go back to work, I still had been nursing the idea of taking a trip to Rome on my own to reward myself. But I still said nothing to Warren because though he was recovering, he was still weak. His need seemed greater.

Warren gradually returned to work at his shop, doing restoration and light framing, until he could regain his strength. At first, he could only work a few hours each day, and I would find him home, lying down already, when I got in from class. His strength increased, however, and his workdays became longer.

After some months, Warren seemed to be doing much better, so we resumed our couples counseling, and at that first session after his hospitalization, I told him, in the counselor's presence, that I wanted to go to

Rome to rest for ten days. Warren blew up. "You can't go! You can't leave me. It's not your decision!"

"It would be good for me to go. I can renew my spirit. Warren, I'm tired; this has all worn me down. It's just for ten days," I pleaded. He was yelling at me.

"You're not going!"

The counselor broke in. "You look fine to me, Warren. You're walking fine; you can go to work every day..."

Then Warren screamed: "I'm not fine!" putting his red face within two inches of the counselor's. "What the fuck do you know about how I feel? I'm sick. He can't go!" I told Warren to back off, which he did.

I was resolved to go to Rome, but I would have to pay the emotional price. I planned the trip four months in the future, but I heard from Warren about how selfish I was every single day.

Warren's workdays became so long that my suspicions grew that he might be using again. I hated to admit this possibility, but he was coming home after nine o'clock, he was up and down all night, and his skin tone was becoming ashen.

I simply asked Warren, in my kitchen one day, if he was using Crystal Meth again.

He said, "Yes." His confirmation so upset me that I grew angry and fearful at the same time. I told him I needed to leave the house. He grabbed my shoulders and said, "Please don't leave!"

I shook my head, and with tears running down my face, blurted out, "You're going to die! You're going to kill yourself, and I don't want to watch it." With that, I was out the front door, and I drove off.

I returned to the house, but I was still distraught.

"You need to get help."

"I'll stop. I can stop on my own," were his last words that day.

I had believed that two months in the hospital and almost losing his life would cause Warren to "hit bottom." But we were back where we had started. I felt powerless and began to listen more attentively to the words I heard at my Al-Anon meeting. "Don't do for others what they can do for themselves," and "Keep the focus on yourself," and "One day at a time." These became my mantra, and though Warren continued to protest, I resolved to take my journey to Rome to take care of myself. I could see no bigger picture at this point.

Part IX: Rome Never Disappoints

My entire focus became my trip to Rome. It was what kept me sane and hopeful.

The Super Shuttle arrived at sunrise. Warren got up to see me off and was kind to me that morning. As I pulled away from the house, I took a deep breath of relief.

On the flight, I slept out of sheer emotional exhaustion. I soon arrived in my city, my second home. I felt safe, finally.

Since my friends in Rome already had houseguests, I arranged lodging at a cheap hotel near the Roman Forum. The room was the size of a closet, but I didn't mind. I was so grateful to be there that I wanted to dance for joy. I looked out the small window at the streets, the ruins, and the restaurants; I already felt better.

The next day I contacted my friend Stefano in Rome,

and we set up a time to meet at a café. When I arrived, I gave Stefano a big hug and met a friend of his. "Mark, this is Rafael." A handsome Latino man with a white sweater and a grey shirt came up and shook my hand.

"You live in Rome, too?" I asked. Rafael said, "Si." Our common language was Italian, so we ordered our coffees and our croissants, and I chatted with Stefano about happy things, saving the sorrowful events for another time. I looked at Rafael. He had a goatee, shaved head, and an athletic body. I found him attractive, but I was careful to avoid his glance in case he noticed my stare. After the coffee, Stefano had to return to work, so Rafael asked if he could catch the bus with me. "Certo," I replied.

Rafael and I got to know each other on the bus, and I asked him which gym he went to. "The one near Campo dei Fiori. Do you know it?" he asked.

"Yes, I have used it."

"I will be there this evening at six if you want to meet up there for a workout," he said. I thought a minute, but I was tired and didn't want to commit. "What are your plans?" he asked. I told him that I intended to go to the ruins in Ostia the next day.

"On Sunday, I will be at Santa Maria in Trastevere at the 10:30 Mass," he said. He reached his stop and got off.

I didn't meet Rafael at 6 p.m. but met Stefano for dinner later. We had been friends for over twenty-five years. Over our meal, I filled him in about my life. "I do think you need to take care of yourself, Mark, because you cannot cure this addiction. Warren may get over this or may never get over it. In the meantime, you have to live your life." I thought about his words as I walked home past the Forum that night. I stopped and looked over the wall into the ancient ruins. I imagined I could hear the conversations of the ancients, like ghosts wandering up the Via Sacra, in all the different ancient languages: slaves, freedmen, patricians, all milling around the temples, markets, and squares. Then I turned and went to my hotel.

The next day I spent in Ostia, exploring the ruins, but I remembered that Rafael told me where he would be on Sunday morning; I started to think that this was an invitation to spend some time together. I would surprise him by showing up at the church.

The following day, I made my way to Santa Maria di Trastevere. Five or six priests came out in green vestments; I then saw Rafael on the other side, in front. It was a children's Mass, so I tried to ignore the kids running around; I tried to focus on spirituality and the experience of God. Rafael kept distracting me. He was so handsome. So manly and intensely focused. Again, I tried not to stare. He never looked in my direction, so I doubted that he knew I was there.

After the service, I sat down to reflect. But after only about a minute, I felt a tap on my shoulder; I turned, and it was Rafael, greeting me with a big smile. "Ciao!" he said. "Can you wait for me? We can go get a coffee." I nodded and waited until he finished chatting with some people.

We left the church together and went to a nearby bar to grab a coffee and a roll. We talked about this and that, and I enjoyed Rafael's friendly and easygoing manner. Though I was attracted to him, I picked up no signals that he was gay, so I was just enjoying the moment of an unplanned day with a possible new friend.

"Would you like to walk down to Santa Cecilia's with me?" he asked.

"That would be great," so we slowly strolled down the cobblestone streets in Trastevere until we reached the church, which was beautiful, with a garden and fountain in the courtyard, but which was, unfortunately, closing when we arrived.

"Damn!" I said.

"That's OK; we can just hang out here for a while in the garden," Rafael suggested. We found some shade.

"Tell me about your life," I said. He made a strange expression, as if "uh-oh," but then he asked, "What would you like to know?" I asked him to tell me about his everyday life in Rome and his life in his country.

In this way, a long three-hour conversation began, in which Rafael shared much of himself. I was sure he was heterosexual when he said, "The biggest sacrifice that I have made is that I want to have a son. But I haven't chosen married life." He told me about his experiences growing up, his dysfunctional family, his girlfriends during high school, his work with youth in the parish in Spain where he helped during the summers, etc. I told him everything about myself except all areas remotely connected to sexuality. "Would you like to sit for a while?" he asked me as he sat on the cement step. I accepted. He had shared so much of himself, and I felt that I had shared so little. If this was going to be a friendship, it had to start with honesty. So, I sat down, and I made a decision that would alienate Rafael.

"I…I want to tell you something, but it is difficult… I want to reveal something to you, but I don't know how you will judge me," I continued.

"I won't judge you at all, Mark," he said warmly.

"OK, I want to tell you that I am more drawn to men than to women, and this is the person that I have discovered that I am." I stopped and looked at him.

Rafael smiled and said, "I am, too."

I said, "Nooo! I don't believe it!" We both revealed to each other a vulnerable part of ourselves that neither of us suspected.

We continued speaking about when we first discovered we were gay, our experiences, our lives in Rome, etc. The afternoon was wearing on, and we were to meet Stefano and friends for a concert that evening. We got up. "Would you like to come to my place?" Rafael asked. We both knew what that meant. I accepted.

Rafael rented a room from a religious organization in Rome; the house was run like a dormitory. His room was bare, with that cold travertine grey floor so standard in Rome. A bed, desk, and small bookshelf made up the furniture.

Before we had the door shut, Rafael practically lunged at me, and we kissed. Hours passed as we kissed so much that my lips got raw and swollen from his goatee. We also made love, danced, listened to music, and reveled in each other's company. I felt totally happy in a way that I could not remember having felt before. I was entirely in the moment. This was real; this was not illusory; this was happiness.

Stefano texted Rafael. "If you are with Mark, be careful!"

Rafael texted back, "Too late!"

I put Warren and the whole painful situation at home out of my mind and found a parenthesis of happiness that I didn't know existed for me with Stefano. It was refreshing.

Part X: What I Want

We arrived at the concert a few minutes late, but quickly found our friends on the right-hand side toward the front. They had saved us seats. I wondered if they could tell how swollen my lips were. We sat down and listened to the sacred music echoing through the ancient church, dancing off the walls, floating from the ceiling, transforming the gilded arches and saintly statues into something alive. I looked over at Rafael, and I felt so happy. But, as minutes passed, a sadness came over me. It was as if I was in the clouds, and I began to sink; I didn't want to descend, but the balloon was deflating, and I could not prop it up. I began to think of Warren, my commitment to him, and my life back in Los Angeles. That began to seem like the real world, and this concert, this church, Rafael and Stefano, these walls were the illusion. From the pinnacle of happiness in the afternoon, my spirit descended to a dark but more realistic place. I could not start something some type of relationship with Rafael; I was already in a relationship. I had to end this thing before it went beyond that one encounter.

After the concert, I knew Rafael wanted to stay the night with me, but I would not have it. I invented some excuse, but the real reason was that I began to regret what I had done with him. I had been unfaithful to Warren, not only sexually but also emotionally. "I will see you tomorrow morning," I told him. He looked discouraged, but what could I do?

I didn't sleep well because I kept thinking of Rafael, then Warren, then Rafael, then Warren, over and over.

Rafael must have seen the writing on the wall the next day because when he saw my face, his smile turned into a frown, and he no longer looked me in the eyes. "Can we take a stroll this morning?" I asked.

"Certo," he replied. For the next few hours, we walked among the glorious monuments of Rome while I explained to him that what had happened between us had to remain an isolated incident, that I could offer him friendship, but nothing more. There was geography; there was the fact that I already had a relationship, there were so many obstacles. Though it felt magical, I admitted, we had to consider real-life on its terms. This was the reasonable next step. Rafael could not disagree more.

"I'm sorry that you are not open to this," he began. "Why put limits? Why not see where it goes? You want to shut it down without even looking at it because you are afraid!" Rafael was angry and hurt, but I couldn't see any other way. "Why can't we just live these last few days with openness, without making any plans, decisions, or projections? Why can't you just be open?" he asked, shaking his head. I wanted to go with what he suggested, but my commitment to Warren tugged at me. We had walked all around historical Rome and ended up near Campo dei Fiori, where we had started that morning. We stood there in front of each other. I wondered if this was the final farewell if he would walk in his direction, and I in mine, our paths never crossing again. I didn't know what to do or say; it had all been said. "Would you like to come to my place for a little bit?" he suggested.

I took a deep breath. "Yes."

When we arrived at Rafael's room, all the boundaries I had set went out the window! Within one minute, we were kissing; within five, we were making love. I could not deny it; I felt happy. I barely knew this feeling. We lay in each other's arms; afterward, it was so easy to be in the present with him. "OK," I said. "I have two more days in Rome, and I want to experience these two days fully with you. I am opening myself completely to this thing between us." I made my decision. I took the leap. Was I crazy? I wanted to prolong the sense of happiness I felt.

Minutes turned to hours, and I had no idea of the passing of time when I was in this state with Rafael. The sun was waning and we were hungry. "Let's grab a bite," he suggested. We went out, and Rome embraced us with a joy that had been lacking that morning.

I had one more full day left in Rome. I would be open to this parenthesis of happiness and consider its repercussions only when I got home.

There was an exposition on Leonardo DaVinci in the city center. The following day, Rafael and I went to see models of his inventions. Because there were few people there, every time we were outside of the guards' eyeshot, Rafael snuck me a kiss or embraced me. I forgot what it was like to feel this way. I wanted to hold his hand and make-believe that we were partners, together for many years, having our lives ahead of us. I was smiling as we left the exposition and made our way to Piazza del Popolo, next to Villa Borghese. Then Rafael proposed an idea. "Why don't we kiss in front of every important monument in Rome"? I shook my head, knowing the homophobia in Rome. "Let's do it!

Not to prove a point for others; let's do it for us!" he said. He was so enthusiastic that I agreed. We made our pilgrimage, sometimes in front of police officers, other times in front of tourists or priests. We kissed each other, just a quick peck, but in front of all the major religious and non-religious sites in Rome.

"Let's have a nice dinner tonight," I suggested. We found an isolated but quaint place off Piazza Navona, where we had a calm conclusion to our adventurous day. "I'm trying not to think about tomorrow," I said.

"Me too," Rafael replied sadly. The following day I was to depart. "Can you stay with me tonight?" I asked. He nodded.

We weren't ready to go to the hotel after dinner, so we walked again. Rome is a city for strolling; that's how the city reveals itself as it changes personalities with the day's hour. It was about nine o'clock, and we found ourselves in Piazza Venezia.

"Why don't we climb the Capitoline?" Rafael suggested. We went to the back of the Victor Emmanuel monument and climbed the stairs up the ancient hill to a park-like area.

"Look," I pointed upwards. "A full moon. It's so bright you can see our shadows!" We stopped near the top of the hill at a rocky outcropping; Rafael climbed on this rock and faced me, the moon to his back. He took my hand and looked me in the eyes.

"Mark, I am going to make a solemn promise to you, on this rock, with the moon as my witness. I swear that my heart will be loyal to you, that I will love you for my whole life, no matter what the circumstances. This rock is the symbol of this love for you, and every time you see this moon, remember that I am binding

116

my heart to yours." Tears came to my eyes as I stepped up on that rock too.

"And I give you my heart," I said as we embraced in joy and sadness.

That night, Rafael stayed over in my little hotel room, in my little bed. I didn't want to fall asleep because I didn't want the night to pass. I wanted to savor every minute with this man and the taste of happiness that I was experiencing. When the alarm did ring at 4:30, I got up reluctantly and prepared to go to the airport.

We rode in silence in the taxi, discreetly holding hands. I longed for the ride to take a long time, but in thirty minutes, we arrived. It was early, so I went through the initial check-in, then Rafael and I went upstairs to have breakfast and to savor the last moments together until we didn't know when. I was using a standby ticket from a friend who worked for the airline. We quickly finished our meal, and Rafael was pensive. We were silent as we got up and moved to a more secluded seating area.

I sat across from him and took his hands. He looked up at me and said, "Mark, don't abandon me." He had tears in his eyes. He then told me the story of a priest friend of his from Columbia who had passed away two years earlier. When it was discovered that the priest had AIDS, he was not even given a public funeral and was abandoned by his friends. Rafael explained that he was living in Europe and was only able to return to Columbia after his friend had died. Rafael said that he went to the grave and prayed. This was his funeral, forsaken by all because of his disease and his being gay. "I do not want to end up like that," he said, tears now rolling down his cheeks. He wiped his tears with the napkins on a nearby table, and I took one of the tear-soaked napkins from him and put it in my pocket. I didn't want to forget this moment.

As the hour drew near for me to go behind the gates, I became emotional; in just a few days, I had begun to love this man, and I didn't want to leave. We both wept as we walked downstairs. I got in line for security clearance. When I was about to cross to the restricted area, I saw Rafael's tear-stained face. Neither of us knew if we would see each other again. Then we both turned and went our separate ways.

Rome always changed me and held some gift; this time, it was meeting Rafael. What this meeting revealed to me was that happiness was not outside of my grasp. Though I had settled for duty, commitment, and rescuing, I still longed for something more. Could happiness be more than a fleeting moment and instead consist of the choices I make?

Part XI: Back Home

I landed in Burbank, and Warren picked me up with Ginger. I was glad to see them both but noticed immediately that my feelings had changed. It seemed like this was now the dream, and Rome was the reality; everything in Los Angeles seemed to be hazy. We spoke about the trip in generalities until we arrived home. I was exhausted, and Warren had no objection to turning in early.

When we lay in bed together and turned out the lights, I became aware of the light of the moon shining on my face through the window; I recalled that night on the Capitoline with Rafael. As Warren dozed off, tears filled my eyes.

In the weeks that followed, Rome became the dream, and the situation with Warren the reality. Warren grew more volatile, at times being the incarnation of sweetness, the next moment turning on me in anger over some trivial matter. I suspected these mood swings were the product of renewed drug use. My suspicion was confirmed when he began to scratch and produced open sores on his arms, which was a symptom of Crystal Meth use. He often remained in the shower for hours as he scrubbed his skin off. The feelings of helplessness returned.

I began talking with Rafael every day on the phone. They were short conversations, but he became my refuge from the harsh reality. I continued my Al-Anon meetings and learned to set limits. One such boundary was that I would not allow myself to be screamed at; every time Warren began to raise his voice, I took my car keys and drove off. This became a common occurrence.

I began to go out onto the balcony every night to look for the moon and the stars. If the moon were visible, I would ask her to communicate my love to Rafael when he looked up. This nightly gaze became my few minutes of peace in an upside-down world.

My birthday was approaching. Every year on that day, I permitted myself to be selfish and to do whatever I wanted. "Let's go to the zoo," I said, and so Warren and I made our plans.

Warren seemed fatigued that February morning as we prepared to leave the house. I took the day off to be free of work and worries. "Are you sure you're up to going?" I asked.

"Yes," he replied, but he didn't seem himself. We drove to the zoo and began to walk to the animal area, but Warren was panting, so we sat near the entrance. After a few minutes, we started again, and once more, he had to sit. He had no energy and was extremely weak. After a few more attempts, I realized this was not going to work. "Why don't I see about getting you a wheelchair?" I suggested. I returned to the entrance and rented a wheelchair, which Warren got into, and I began to push. But the pathways in the zoo were hilly, and I was huffing and puffing. "This isn't going to work either," I said. "Why don't we take the train?" We could thus encircle the zoo while sitting down.

Fortunately, the zoo train was a short distance away. We boarded it, and it chugged around the perimeter. I glanced over at Warren, who was falling asleep. I put my hand on his leg to wake him. He opened his eyes, but he dozed off again a minute later and began leaning dangerously outside the train car. This would not work either. "Warren, I think we should go home. You're falling asleep, and you might fall out of the train." He didn't object as we slowly made our way to the car and soon arrived home.

Arriving back at the house, we sat out on the balcony overlooking the sunny view of Hollywood. Warren began to cry. "I wanted so badly to give you this day," he began. "I'm so sorry, honey. I love you so much, and I couldn't give you this day." I felt so bad for him that tears poured down my cheeks also. I didn't know what to do or say to make things better.

My birthday thus became a day of caretaking. I did this without resentment because it was second nature. But it was not what I had hoped for.

The happiness that I tasted in Rome faded, and again, I felt that I had no choices. Timothy played a minor role in Warren's life, and Warren couldn't function on his own. He needed me, and I could not abandon him. I had to put my needs aside and fulfill my commitment to him. I believed that this was more important than my happiness.

Part XII: The Last Straw

My life with Warren continued rotating between tension and calm, never knowing what I would have to face when I got home. One day, however, Warren did not return from work at the usual time. At six o'clock, he was not there. I called his office and cell phone, but no answer. At seven, still no Warren. By eight, I was agitated and called one of his tenants living near the shop where he worked. "Warren left hours ago," was the reply. When he had not shown up by nine, I called the hospital and asked if Warren had been admitted. "No one here by that name," was the answer.

I was becoming frantic and started to wonder whether Warren was alive or dead. Why no word? What could have happened?

It was past 11 p.m. when the phone rang, and I ran to get it. "Mark, this is Warren. I'm in jail. Can you come to bail me out?" he said. My heart plunged. "In jail for what?" Warren paused. "Driving under the influence and drug possession." I felt anger and sadness at the same time. I decided not to react. I hung up, got in my car, and drove down to the jail area where there were bail bondsmen. As I was on the road, I said out loud, "This is not the way I want to live."

The process of bailing Warren out took longer than expected, and it was the next day before he was released. When I picked him up, his arms were covered with oozing sores from scratching. I was so furious that I said little as we made our way back to the house. By the time we got home, I had decided. "Warren, I need some time apart. I'm going to sleep downstairs." Warren didn't react as I expected but replied, "I thought you would say something like that."

I set up a boundary; that night and the next day, I would stay in the apartment on the second level, and Warren would stay upstairs. Warren was soon testing and violating the boundary, finding excuses to come downstairs. One night I was sound asleep and was jolted awake by Warren's angry voice. "I had a terrible nightmare! I'm up there all alone! You have no compassion! You're so selfish!" he shouted at me as he stomped through my apartment at 3 in the morning. I was shaken and didn't feel safe. He left, but I lay awake the rest of the night.

I kept the door ajar between our two levels because we shared custody of Ginger, and she would cry and whimper if she could not come into my apartment. But the drawback of the arrangement was that Warren was coming down the stairs and into my unit all the time.

I was about to go on break from work when Rafael invited me to come to Spain, where he was living at this time. I felt guilty about making such a trip without Warren, but he was still taking drugs and doing whatever he wanted to do, so why couldn't I do what I wanted to do? These were my thoughts when I called Rafael and told him, "I am coming."

Warren, of course, threw a fit at the idea of my

leaving. He continued to repeat to me how selfish I was to abandon him in his hour of need. However, I had had enough. His arrest had signaled to me that he could very well live with this addiction for the rest of his life. But I wasn't finished living yet; I had so much more I wanted to do, see, and experience.

Warren said he would begin going to a 12-Step Program, but it felt too late. I no longer believed in his recovery.

I was confused about my life's direction and was feeling that I had no power over it. Spain would give me some space, a pause, perspective, I hoped. I kept away from Warren as much as possible that week preceding my departure to minimize his berating me. Then, early one morning, Super Shuttle came and whisked me off.

Warren's arrest shattered my belief that the drugs were a phase that he would pass through and that the "real Warren" would eventually emerge. After his surgery, he was not getting better but was sinking even deeper into addiction. I began to realize that I did not want to live like this. Though I did not yet know how to extricate myself from the situation, I decided that this is not the life that I would live. I would begin to make my own choices and focus on taking care of myself.

Part XIII: Happiness is a Decision

I arrived in Madrid the next day; I felt so happy to be in this new place, far away from the awful situation at home. When I met Rafael at our Pensione (Bed and Breakfast) near the gay section of town, we made love with passion. Everything else faded.

I did not call Warren on the first, second, or third day. I didn't know what to expect on the other end, and I didn't want to risk feeling bad.

Rafael and I spent our days at Madrid's museums and the evenings at the various gay venues in the city. At times I worried about the situation at home, but I kept repeating to myself, "Be present where your feet are." I wanted to live in the moment and leave tomorrow until tomorrow.

I was happy with Rafael and found myself smiling all the time. Why could I not live my whole life this way, I wondered.

"Why don't we go to Barcelona?" I asked Rafael a few days into the trip. We went to an internet café and looked up lodging; eventually, we found a small pensione just off Las Ramblas, the main thoroughfare. We booked it and set off the following day.

We arrived at dusk; we made our way across the city and found our small pensione on the second floor of a commercial building. Someone was waiting to check us in. "You must pay up front because there is no one on duty here," they told us. The facility consisted of six rooms and two shared bathrooms, with no front desk or way to contact the manager should there be a problem. I didn't like what I saw. Having no other choices, I paid for the four nights, and we unpacked our things in our tiny room.

We explored Barcelona at night, with its incredible architecture and exciting street life. We took a long walk and found ourselves in a medieval-l looking courtyard where we sat to enjoy the atmosphere and each other. I breathed deeply of this place with Rafael at my side.

The next day, we decided to take a double-decker tourist bus to see the city highlights. There were fewer museums than in Madrid, but the Gaudi architecture was something out of a storybook. We were anxious to see La Sagrada Familia church, partially completed but quickly taking form. As we got off the bus, we heard the announcement: "This cathedral has been many years in the making and is constructed using only the offerings of the faithful." I listened to this with skepticism as we got in line to pay our ten Euro entrance fee.

"Where does all this money go?" I asked Rafael. "Maybe they are delaying construction just so they can keep collecting it," I continued. Notwithstanding my sarcasm, however, the cathedral was awe-inspiring. The columns rose out of the ground like great tree trunks, branching out into leaves supporting the ceiling. It was amazing.

It started to drizzle as we finished touring the cathedral, so we made our way back to Las Ramblas. The area was dirty and crowded. I didn't see the beauty described in the tourist books, and soon we had had enough. "Let's get a bite to eat," I suggested. We found a sit-down place, reasonably priced, where we had a lovely Spanish meal. As we took our time eating and enjoying ourselves, the drizzle turned into rain. By the time we paid our bill, it was a downpour.

We were soaked when we entered our room. Though the bed was made, it didn't look like the room had been cleaned. When Rafael pulled back the bedspread, his pants were inside the sheets. The house cleaner had simply pulled the sheets up, covering the clothes that had been lying on the bed. No other cleaning had been done, not even of the bathroom, which we shared with others. "This is the worst place I have stayed in!" I said.

Rafael agreed but added, "At least we are together."

There was a thunderclap and even heavier rain, so we resigned ourselves to staying in that night. The reception on the TV was so poor that Rafael turned it off. He sat down facing me, and on that night, in that grimy pensione in Barcelona, we had a conversation that changed my life.

"Are you happy, Mark?" Rafael asked.

"Right now, I'm extremely happy," I said.

"But what about with your life? Are you happy with your life?" I paused but didn't answer. "Why is that such a difficult question for you?" he asked.

"I guess I feel trapped. I feel like I have to take care of Warren and that he will fall apart without me."

Rafael asked, "As long as you have been taking care of him, has he stopped using drugs?"

I had to admit, "No, but he has only been using for five years, and…"

Rafael interrupted me. "Do you hear what you are saying? Do you hear yourself? You are so far inside of this that you can't even see what's going on here. You think that five years is not a lot of time to be addicted and that he is going to get over it soon? Mark, come on! I lost my oldest brother to alcohol. If you stay with Warren, I hope it is because you accept the situation as it is, not holding onto this insane hope that he will change. Your whole life will pass you by as you wait and hope. If you tell me that you want to stay with Warren and accept and are content with this situation, then I am happy for you. At least that is realistic. But if you are hoping for a change, it is yourself that you are deluding." His words stung, and I wanted to change the subject. But I didn't. I realized that I had been avoiding these things that I knew were true. "I don't think you will ever leave Warren," he continued. "If you didn't leave him immediately after his arrest, you will never leave him. Do you know who has suffered so much about this? Stefano. He loves you so and is concerned about you. And he also thinks that you will never leave Warren." Stefano was my dear friend whom I had known since my time in the seminary.

I hated hearing these words. The rain continued to pour; the building shook with thunder.

"So why do you stay with me?" I asked Rafael. He got off the bed.

"That is an excellent question. Why do I stay with you? It is because I love you without any conditions, whether you stay with Warren or not. But I do want you to be true to yourself and be clear on why you are staying. Stay if you accept the situation as it is. Don't stay because you hope for him to change, which probably will not happen." I hated hearing this, hated, hated, hated it! But he was right. Every word was on target.

He finished by saying: "In the end, Mark, you are going to have to choose between yourself and him."

I felt cornered by the truth with no escape. If I went to the right, I would be blocked; the same if I went to the left. I had to face this situation head-on. "I will leave Warren," I said. Rafael shook his head.

"If you do, do so for yourself. But I don't believe it," he said coldly.

"I will," and with that, our conversation ended.

Warren had called me several times. I didn't pick

up, but the next day I responded. He was irate. "Why haven't I heard from you? I thought something had happened to you! You could have at least called when you arrived." I was being berated, and my attempts at justifying why I hadn't called were brushed aside. I listened quietly, then as calmly as possible, got off the phone. Rafael looked at me admonishingly, as if I should not have picked up the phone. He shook his head. I was the one, however, who had to deal with Warren, not Rafael, and no communication would only make the situation more explosive. But I felt pressure from Rafael to handle things his way, which made me uncomfortable.

My resolve to leave Warren was firm, though I had no idea when or how I would do it. I began to realize, however, that if I did not leave him now when things had gotten so bad, I would never leave him. This was my last chance to get my life back.

Rafael and I returned to Madrid. I often found myself distracted, however, thinking about how I would communicate my decision to Warren. "Be present where your feet are," I kept repeating to myself. We went to Escorial and other sites, which I enjoyed, though my anxiety over my impending breakup was just under the surface.

I was good at denial; it had become part of my daily life with Warren. My beliefs were a form of denial: the drugs are a phase, he will become the man I imagine, he cannot live without me. It took another person, Rafael, to make me face the truth. Looking back, it seems the rainy night in Barcelona was not a fluke but part of a greater plan to rescue me from the depths into which I was sinking.

Part XIV: Him or Me

I flew home to Los Angeles with a sense of dread. Because Warren was at an AA meeting, I took a shuttle to the house. When I got home, I found a vase of flowers from him on the kitchen counter and Ginger on the bed, wagging her tail and barking in happiness. The flowers were like a knife. When I approached the bed to pet Ginger, I burst into tears; I would probably lose her or seldom see her. I let the tears flow as I put things away, then crawled into bed as Ginger continued to lick my tears away. When Warren came in a few hours later, I pretended I was asleep, not knowing how to greet or approach him.

We had planned a trip to Hawaii the following month; I thought we could go on the trip and enjoy our time together. Then when we returned, I would sit him down and have "the talk."

That following day, I greeted Warren normally and gave him a big hug. I tried to act as if everything was the same, though everything inside of me was different. Carrying out this decision would be hard. It would be easier to leave things as they were. I had to fight to regain myself.

A few days later, we were driving together to church when Warren asked me how my trip went and how it made me feel about us. I wanted to wait, but this was a window of opportunity. Though I had rehearsed what I would say a hundred times, my mind went blank. I wanted to make my point without hurting his feelings. Was that an impossible task? I would try anyway. "I thought that we have evolved into more of a friendship, so we should just accept that instead of fighting it."

"You mean you don't want to be in a relationship with me?" he said, in disbelief.

"I wanted to talk with you about this after our trip to Hawaii…"

He broke in. "I don't want to go to Hawaii with you! Cancel the trip. How could you do this to me!" He began to rant as we pulled up to the church.

"Can we do this afterward?" I asked. He agreed, and we walked in. My heart was in turmoil.

Warren's anger continued to escalate on the drive home. Once we did arrive at the house, he stomped upstairs and slammed the door. I wanted to make things better, but I had no idea how to fix this situation.

There was a man we knew from church named William, who had a partner at the time. Apparently, William had an interest in Warren because that evening, Warren came downstairs and told me he would invite William over to stay the night with him. He looked for my reaction. "If that's what you want to do, what can I say?" He took up the phone and called William, but in the end told him, "It is too soon for this," and he hung up. Warren began to cry and came toward me so that I might hold him, which I did. He kept repeating. "Please don't leave me!"

I was torn between wanting to take care of Warren's feelings and sticking to my decision. I silently repeated that I needed to choose between him and me. Even if it killed me, I needed to choose myself.

Over the next few days, I avoided the house as much as possible because a knife could cut through the tension and sadness. But I could not stay away all day, and I would return when I no longer had anything to occupy me. One afternoon Warren came downstairs and said he wanted to talk. Tears rolled down his face as he told me how sorry he was for everything that had transpired, that he would make amends, that things would be different, and he would make it up to me. "Please, honey, don't go away! Please don't leave me!" he pleaded.

"I don't know what to say," were the words that came out of my mouth. Warren then dropped to the floor and wrapped his arms around my legs, sobbing, "Please give me a second chance! Please, Mark, please!" It broke my heart. I had never known such pain before.

I could only soften my approach. "Warren, we don't know the future. Let's just take this break. Maybe we will both heal and give it another try." My compromising position seemed to console him. What did I know about how this would play out, I asked myself? The rest of the day was spent in relative but uncertain, calm.

The next day Warren phoned me from upstairs with a slurring voice. "Mark, I just want to let you know that I love you and that I don't want to live without you. I took an overdose of pills and decided to end my life." I put down the phone and ran upstairs, finding him in bed with his eyes closed. He opened them and said, "Everything is getting dark." I grabbed the phone and dialed 911 as he begged me not to. This was complete insanity, I told myself. When the buzzer rang below, I went downstairs to let the police in, and we went up the three flights to where Warren's unit was. When we arrived, Warren was not there. We looked downstairs, in the closet, in the backyard, and still no Warren.

The police stayed about half an hour, and during that time, Warren called. The officer asked to speak with him to make sure he was all right. "He said that he just wanted to scare you, that he only took two sleeping pills, and that he will come back once we leave. If there is any other problem, call us, and we will return right away." I thanked them for showing up, and we all cleared out so that Warren could come out of hiding. I later found him in his bed asleep.

The next day I was the brunt of Warren's anger as he yelled at me about how unfeeling and selfish I was. I left the house shaking; I found refuge in a Starbucks in the neighborhood. I still had another month off from work, and staying in this situation with Warren for all that time would be too much. I had a crazy idea. I had another voucher for a free flight to Europe; I took out my cell phone and called my friend Stefano. "Stefano, things are so crazy at home. Can I come to stay with you in Rome for a few weeks?

"When?"

"I can come next week."

"Great. I'll see you then."

Immediately afterward, I called Rafael and told him of my plan. "I'll meet you there. I'll find a way," he said. It was set. I just needed to let Warren know that I would be gone.

"You're not going to Rome," he screamed when I told him of my plan. "I need you now! You can't go!" I would be leaving in five days, but Warren's anger grew daily. He began to become more verbally and physically abusive, coming downstairs to my unit and grabbing my arm tightly, so tightly it started to bruise. He would not let go unless I repeated after him, "I am a dictator because I am going to Rome." He then announced that he was inviting William to stay over that night. I shrugged but didn't say a word. I knew that whatever I said could set him off, so it was better just to keep my mouth shut and say nothing.

My caretaking and attempts to rescue Warren had backfired on me. I had focused so much on him that I forgot how to care for myself. When I decided to leave the relationship and began to carry out this decision, I felt torn in two directions. Warren's dire need of me pulled against my desire to have my life back. I felt so powerless and terrible about my decision, but I didn't doubt for a moment that it was the right one. I imagined my new life as being on the other side of a torrential river; if I could just get to the other side, I would be safe.

Part XV: Out of the Depths

Though this trip to Rome didn't resolve or make the situation at home better, it gave me the serenity to move forward with my decision and to not be swayed by Warren's needs. The days in the magical city with Stefano and Rafael were calm and nourishing and, though I dreaded my return home, I was ready when two weeks had passed.

On my return to Los Angeles, my task would be to end my relationship with Warren. There were some complications because we owned the triplex together, sharing the mortgage and other bills. We also shared our dog; Warren was on my health insurance and our lives overlapped countless ways. I hoped that the fact that Warren had immediately picked up a new boyfriend would be a buffer to his wrath.

By the time I got home, it was late, and I was tired. I

walked in and stood there, shocked. My unit had been stripped. Every piece of artwork had been removed from the walls. Every piece of furniture except the sofa and bed and every object that was tied to Warren was gone. A chime doorbell was unique and came with the house; only wires were left jutting out of the wall. I went to my bedroom to check the door connecting my unit with the one upstairs; there were now three locks on the door, and they had been reversed so that Warren could lock the door from his side, but I could not. I found a board to jam the door closed so I could feel safe during the night. I crept around quietly so as not to be heard and slipped into my bed.

The following day, I took a closer look around. Warren must have hired a whole crew to come to move things. The large, potted plants outside of my door were now gone, patio furniture disappeared, the dining table was missing. Even a framed picture was given to us by a parishioner at our church, which said, "God bless this house," was removed.

I avoided running into Warren over the following days and went about refurnishing my unit with used furniture. In a few days, my place was livable again and, for once, reflected more my personality than Warren's.

The taking of belongings, sealing the door between our units, and the fact that Warren now had a new boyfriend completed our separation. The relationship was now over. I no longer had to ride the rollercoaster. I could now move forward with my life and even experience that happiness that I had glanced but not yet possessed.

Part XVI: Lessons Learned and Repeated

When I met Warren, he was already in a relationship. I never asked myself where this situation might lead; I simply followed an attraction. I thought that I could control my feelings, but I experienced emotional hardship as I fell in love with someone who was not free to commit. Dating someone already in a relationship was putting me in a second-class position and affirmed that I didn't deserve someone who could give a complete commitment. This lowered my self-esteem and set me up for a codependent relationship as I put another above my own needs.

I believed that I could date a man already in a relationship and keep my feelings under control, but this proved false. As friendship evolved into a sexual relationship, emotions soon followed, and my attachment to Warren was more than I had expected. Dating a man who was already in a relationship was not something I could do and remain healthy.

I also held onto the belief that loving someone was the same as loving his potential. I loved Warren, but I was in love with the man I imagined he could be. I gradually realized that the surest predictor of future behavior was past patterns. As I moved from dating to a relationship with Warren, I experienced the same abuse and addiction patterns that were part of his former relationship. Yet I lived on hope, longing for the day when Warren might grow out of this. My life was put on hold as I waited for him to change.

Besides waiting, I believed that I could change Warren. If only I could think of the right thing to say or the right action to take, perhaps I could lure him out of addiction. I would try to come up with ways to make Warren change so that I could feel OK. This mindset was an illusion, imagining that I could change him or had some sort of power over him. I learned that those faced with an addicted partner or family member are often drawn into this way of thinking, which robs one of serenity because all of one's thoughts and energy are spent on trying to rescue the one who is sinking into addiction.

There was a much simpler thought process that I eventually arrived at, which was a simple question to myself: Does this work for me, or not? Framing the question in these terms took the focus off Warren and placed it back on me. At that point, I realized that I had choices.

Did I love Warren, or was I in love with my idea of who he should be? It was not an easy question to answer, but what did become apparent was that they were not the same thing. Rafael was on target when he said that unless I could fully embrace Warren's struggle with drug abuse and stop focusing on a blissful future, I had no business being with him. Could I be happy with the person that he was and with the life I had with him? It took a long time and much pain and disappointment for me to be able to finally say no. I could not be happy in this relationship, nor could I accept him with his addiction. The choice to leave was the only sane step.

I was new to the world of addiction, and I believed Warren's promise never to use Crystal again. I thought that it only took a decision to stop using. When one promise after another was broken, I came to see addiction as a disease that could be arrested but not cured. A decision could be the beginning of a recovery journey, but it was not sufficient to overcome substance dependence. I would learn this the hard way by traveling that road with Warren until I realized that his addiction was killing him and destroying me. To learn to move the focus from him and place it back on me was an excruciating process, but it was the only way to achieve emotional health. Warren would have to take care of Warren; he did get a new boyfriend within a week. Mark would have to focus on developing a healthy relationship with himself.

The classic sign of codependency is when one becomes so focused on another that one's sense of self becomes enmeshed in the other. A codependent personality can be drawn to an addict or broken person like a fly to honey. Rescuing someone else can give a sense of self-worth, meaning, and even a sense of fulfillment for a while, which is why the codependent is drawn. But it never leads to happiness because it is based on the illusion that one has the power to change another and that the codependent person cannot live without the other.

When I was with Warren, I realized that I had lost the sense of my own life and had simply taken on Warren's. My needs seemed so minor compared with the drama of his addiction. Calming his anxiety seemed more important than my peace of mind. Making time for him overshadowed cultivating my interests. My friendships shrank in importance, and some were lost. My life became his life.

Once I realized that this situation was destroying me, it was clear that it would be a struggle to regain myself. During those days and weeks of the separation process, I would imagine myself as a soldier from the ancient world, walking across a battlefield with his sword and shield in hand, his gaze fixed ahead on the impending battle. On the ground surrounding him were the dead and wounded; some were reaching up to him for help. But he did not turn his gaze down or stop to comfort those around him. Instead, he looked ahead at the battle, gaze fixed. This is the image that gave me the strength to fix my gaze on the prize, which was to get my life back.

I left the relationship with a mind and heart full of lessons. I saw where dating somebody in a relationship could lead. I realized that loving someone's potential is different from loving him. I learned that overcoming an addiction is a life long journey. Finally, though rescuing may look like love, it is not love at all, and codependency is as lethal as the drug is to the addict.

The last word on Warren, however, is that it was not all loss and suffering. It was through him that I learned to embrace my past. He was the instrument by which I began to reconcile the man I had been with the one I was becoming. He helped me realize that the life of the spirit did not have to be opposed to that of the flesh, and that the road that I had traveled up to now was valid, unique, and beautiful. For this, I remain grateful.

Chapter 4: Long Distance Dream

Love is an attempt to change a piece of
a dream world into reality.
Henry David Thoreau

Beliefs:
> A relationship is destiny: I am "meant" to be with this person.
> Love means financially supporting the other.
> Love makes two people compatible.

Part I: Meant to be with Him

I was now free to pursue a relationship with Rafael, but geography was a challenge because he had moved back to Columbia. I had vacation days at Christmas time, but the airfare to his city was $800, and I was $800 short. "Trust the angels," he suggested, so I put the whole affair in God's hands, and we kept in touch.

During this period, my feelings for Rafael grew. "You fill me," I told him one night, which sounded better in Italian than in English. I thought about Rafael most of the time as we called each other two or three times a day. I imagined what it would be like if he could move to the United States, as a university professor, and we could make a life together. Or would I eventually move to Europe to be with him? Or would we establish a life in South America? I was open to anything and was sure that we were destined to be together.

Circumstances confirmed this certainty: the bank refunded me $800 that was left in the joint account I had held with Warren. Now I was free to travel to Rafael.

I had never been to South America before, and I was surprised how short the connecting flight was from Miami. Customs and baggage claim took forever, but once I saw Rafael in the receiving area, it was all worth it. I had the sense that this was "meant to be." How else could I explain the money coming my way and, back even further, meeting Rafael at that precise point in my life?

I had caught a bug on the flight, and by the time I had arrived at my destination, I had a sinus headache. I was determined not to allow my cold to define my trip, but I warned Rafael after we hugged in the airport. "No kissing on lips for a few days till I'm over this, OK?" We held hands as we sped off.

I didn't sleep well that night because, despite my efforts, my cold got worse. I had so looked forward to these days with Rafael, but I preferred to be at home when sick. "Do you want to go downstairs and get some tea?" he asked.

"Yes." Over steaming cups, he told me that Stefano, who was visiting from Italy, invited us to dinner that night at a friend's house, a wealthy woman he had known for years. "Do you think you are up for that?" he asked. "I'll say yes right now." I didn't want to miss out.

That evening my cold grew worse, but I felt

obligated to go to this dinner because I had accepted. "Can we get out of this engagement?" I asked Rafael.

"We have to go now. It's too late to back out," he said. I went along with this against my better judgment. I placed more importance on keeping everyone happy than taking care of myself.

We reached our destination at 7:30, and I figured that I could make it through dinner if we left by 9.

Nine o'clock came and went, and there was no dinner served; the group of six people sat in the living room, sipping on drinks, while I grew more feverish by the minute. I whispered to Rafael that I was becoming more ill; he nodded but didn't move. It was ten o'clock when he received a phone call and used that as an excuse for us to leave. By this time, I had a fever and only wanted to get into bed.

As we left the house, Rafael explained that the call was from a friend who was having a crisis in her marriage that evening. Rafael wanted to stop by just for a minute. I hesitated but acquiesced.

We arrived at her home and rang the bell; when Maria opened the door, she was crying. The couple had been arguing, yelling, and fighting for hours.

Rafael disappeared into the back room with Maria, and they spoke for thirty minutes. When he came out, I stood to leave; he then motioned for me to sit down as he went to talk with the husband.

As I sat on their sofa waiting for Rafael, I began to wonder about my belief that we were meant to be together. How well did I know Rafael? What place did I fill in his life? Hours later, when we arrived home and were finally in bed, these questions remained in my mind that night and for the rest of my trip.

Part II: Words Versus Actions in Columbia

In March, I flew down to Columbia to revisit Rafael. This time I brought gifts.

In the preceding months, we had joked with each other. "I'm not your rich American uncle," and he would reply, "And I'm not your rich Columbian uncle either!" The words expressed an unwillingness to be financially dependent on the other, but my actions spoke otherwise.

Rafael told me that his computer was breaking down. "Let me see whether I can find one here on sale," I had offered.

"But I don't want you to spend," he objected.

"I will not spend what I cannot afford," I said. I purchased the computer and packed it in my suitcase.

In our telephone discussions, Rafael told me of a class he began teaching at the university for which he needed a digital projector for his lectures. I already had a projector that I was no longer using. "What if I brought you my projector?" I asked. "No, you might need it. I wish there were another way. I really could use one. But don't worry about it. Patience." I didn't want to see him in need, so I purchased a projector for him.

I was equating love with taking care of Rafael's material needs without questioning his motives or mine. I was rescuing again.

Rafael knew nothing about either gift, which I would surprise him with when I visited. However, he did mention that he had to wait for busses all the time because he had no car and that he needed to purchase a vehicle. He had spoken with his sister about borrowing money for the down payment. Besides this, a friend of his in a bank was working to secure him a loan. He needed about $4,000 for the down payment, and he described how terrible he felt in asking his sister for this money, because she was already in financial need herself. "Why don't I front you that money? You can pay me back whenever you can," I said. Again, for me, giving was the same thing as love, and I did not hesitate.

A few weeks later, when I visited Rafael, he had his car, and he was overjoyed when I gave him his gifts. I was happy that I could make his life easier but was still unaware that my actions were setting up a situation that would be difficult to change.

A few days later, Rafael and I headed to a chapel where we were going to the Sunday service. On the way, we were chatting; he used a word in Italian that I was unfamiliar with at a certain point. "I don't understand." Suddenly, without warning, he burst out. "You NEVER listen! You are always inside of your head! You're always thinking of something else when people are talking to you! I'm not going to repeat what I said because you weren't listening!" he continued.

I broke in. "Rafael, I didn't understand the meaning of your words because my Italian is rusty. That's why I asked you to repeat yourself."

He continued his attack. "That's just your excuse! You don't listen! You never listen!" I felt so angry that I wanted to get out of the car and considered telling him to let me out. But then what would I do, I thought, in a foreign country. We arrived at the church, and he went to the front while I went to sit toward the middle. I was furious, but I calmed down as the service began.

143

Once the Mass was over, Rafael returned to being his usual, jolly self as if nothing had occurred. I was at sea; these outbursts, followed by normal and even affectionate behavior, echoed my experience with Warren.

Some days later, I was in the kitchen putting groceries away while he was in his office. I had the back door open to cool down the room. When I turned, a soldier and a woman, a married couple, were standing at the doorway; they asked to speak to Rafael about their son. I asked them to wait outside, leaving the door ajar and fetched him. As the couple began to discuss something about their child with Rafael, I withdrew to the other side of the house. When he finished with them, Rafael entered the room and was livid. "How could you leave them there with the door open? They could be robbers for all you know! I can't believe you!"

I looked at him in disbelief. "They were a couple asking for you, so I called you. What was so wrong?"

He shook his head. "You are slow, aren't you? You can never leave the door open with strangers around. Can't you figure that out?" Now I was mad, but there was no persuading Rafael because he always had to be right. This I knew by now.

As he became even angrier and I could not get a word in, I stated, "I am not going to participate in this conversation because I am not going to allow myself to be spoken to in this way." Then I stopped talking. He taunted me and tried to draw me into an argument, but I refused. Whatever I said would be rejected, so why bother speaking, I thought.

A few days later, Rafael came to the house with a huge flower bouquet. "I want to give you this to express how much I love you," he said. I was confused about the contradictory behavior.

I was bewildered by the dynamic between Rafael and me during this visit. But I was not ready to give up on the relationship. The belief in this relationship as something "meant to be" had catapulted me into the life of someone whom I didn't know or understand. My financial support of Rafael came with no strings attached, but I started to wonder not only if this man loved me as he said he did, but if he even liked me. Yet, I still didn't feel I had enough evidence to understand what was going on between us.

Perhaps more time together would clarify things. "What do you think of spending time somewhere else next time, say Costa Rica?" I asked Rafael.

"That would be great, but what about the money? I earn so little; you know that," he objected. "Let me figure it out."

To pay for these gifts and visits to Rafael, I was working 11-hour days and some Saturdays. This situation was wearing on me. I was exhausted in the evenings, and I used the weekends to sleep. I didn't have the time or energy to cultivate any local friendships. My life became focused on the next time Rafael and I would be together.

Part III: Give and Give in Costa Rica

Even though the happiness that I expected to flow from my relationship was proving elusive, I was still bound by my belief that, somehow, Rafael and I were destined to be together. The role he played in the steps I took to regain my life and leave Warren, the similarities in our backgrounds, and the friendships we held in common; all of this seemed to add up to some greater plan. I hung on even though Rafael was not turning out to be the man he had appeared initially.

Over the following months, I worked hard to earn money for Costa Rica. I would pay for my flight and the hotels, while Rafael would cover his flight and help with meals. I looked forward to this trip because my past visit was so wrought with stress and doubts. Perhaps this time together would clear things up and enable us to have the harmonious relationship that I longed for.

A few days before my departure, Rafael told me that he was fighting a cold and hoped it would not interfere with our plans. I assured him I would take care of him if he needed anything; the important thing was that we were together.

I met Rafael at the hotel in San Juan, where we had a lovely room; it was off-season, so there were few guests at this gay establishment. We embraced each other and kissed, on the side of the mouth, to avoid contagion. I felt happy to see him. "Do you want to look around?" I suggested. We then went outside and explored the pool, Jacuzzi, bar, and small gym.

"This place is perfect," Rafael stated.

We planned on going out to dinner that evening and asked for directions to the nearest decent eating establishment. "I'll wait for you on the terrace," I said while Rafael dressed. I went out and looked down at the pool and garden. It was a serene place.

A few minutes later, Rafael walked out with a serious expression on his face. "Mark, I wanted to wait to do this, but I can't. You know how I am," he said; I had no idea what he was leading into. "Mark, I don't have much. I wish I could give you so much more," he said as he got down on one knee. He reached up and took my hand, and slipped a gold ring on my finger. "Please take this ring as a sign of my love for you. I promise always to love and be near you, be loyal to you, and share my life with you. Take this ring as a sign that I give you my heart." Then I drew him up and held him close. I wondered, however, about the meaning of his gesture. The ring symbolized a level of commitment that we had not discussed.

Over the next few days, I knew that Rafael was pushing himself as we visited the museums and cultural sights in the capital; it came as no surprise that, by the time we arrived in Arenal, he was sick with a fever. The area was beautiful, at the base of an active volcano, but Rafael was confined to our room.

Three days later, we left Arenal to visit the cloud forest area of Costa Rica. By the time we got there, Rafael was even more ill. We had a small cabin, and he got into bed while I went out to look for some hot soup. He ate the soup and some bread, accepted an aspirin, and then returned to bed. When he awoke the following day, he was feeling well.

When we took a guided tour of the cloud forest, Rafael was better, but I started to feel a scratchy sensation in my throat. I hoped it was nothing and pushed it from my mind.

The last part of our Costa Rican adventure was at a gay resort in its southern region. This part was the culmination of our trip and was the most expensive lodging I had booked. However, when we were shown our room, we were disappointed because it was not much bigger than a closet. "We can give you a discount on a suite with a kitchen if you like because we are not full," the proprietor offered. I made the calculations and nodded to Rafael. "Let's do it!" and we thus ended up in a large beautiful apartment with a bedroom and full kitchen.

The resort's pool and Jacuzzi area were clothing optional, but it appeared that the resort was mostly empty. "There will be more people coming over the weekend," the manager told us.

I set to work unpacking my suitcase while Rafael lay on the bed and turned on the TV. He loved watching television and became so mesmerized that he was incommunicado. "Rafael, do you want to get something to eat?" I asked.

"No," was his response as he was laughing at a TV program. When his program was over, he came into the kitchen.

"Mark, I'm starving. Do we have anything to eat?" he asked. "Didn't you hear me ask you about getting food?" He hadn't.

He became suddenly animated and changed the subject. "Mark, we need to rent a car!" I hesitated due to the expense. I was already paying for the hotel and food; renting a car would put me over the edge. Plus, it seemed to me that we were within walking distance of everything. I shook my head.

"I don't think we need or can afford a car. Why don't we see if we can do without for now because we just got here."? He grew angry. "No, I want a car. I want us to have freedom to go places. We can split the expense. Or I'll just pay for it!" he said. I shrugged. "I don't think we need a car, but if you want to rent one,

I can't stop you." Rafael was exasperated that I did not support his idea.

"Just help me do the renting part, OK?" We got up and went to the office, and began the process of renting a four-wheel drive. There was tension between us over this car, but I was determined not to let it ruin my day. He expected me to pay for the car rental and seemed angry as he went through the rental procedure.

"I don't know how I will pay for this when I get the bill on my credit card," he said.

I was becoming more ill as the day grew on, and by nightfall, I could no longer deny that I had the same symptoms as Rafael. "I'm going to lie down for a bit," I said.

"Me, too," and we both rested, but Rafael got up and left the room.

I slept for three or four hours, then got up, made some tea, and wondered where Rafael was. Not wanting to watch Spanish television, I left the apartment and walked down to the pool. It was deserted. There was also a secluded Jacuzzi area several levels down among the trees, and I walked down to that area and saw two heads in the Jacuzzi. Walking further, I saw Rafael and a hotel patron that I had seen earlier in the day. It struck me as curious that they were together there, and when I approached, I saw that they were both naked. When I approached, Rafael said, "Come on in." I hesitated, turned, and walked back up to the apartment. I felt confused, jealous, and angry.

A brief time later, Rafael arrived with an irritated expression. "What's wrong with you?" he demanded. "I was just there talking; nothing was going on. This guy felt so bad he just left. What are you, like the jealous wife?" I looked at him and realized that he was not interested in anything I had to say. "We can talk about this, calmly, another time," I said. Rafael tried to egg me on, but I refused to discuss it further because his only objective was to try to make me admit the error of my ways.

We didn't talk about it before another issue came up that I couldn't avoid.

I wasn't feeling well, so I got ready for bed; Rafael was tired also, so we lay down. Because I slept with a CPAP machine, having sleep apnea, I woke up every few hours, having to blow my nose, put the mask on again, and then fall asleep.

I awoke at 5 a.m. because the television was on. Rafael was sitting on the bed, chuckling at the Spanish variety show he was watching. "Rafael," I said, but he did not turn or answer. He was mesmerized. I switched my position and put a pillow over my head to muffle the sound to try to sleep. But it was no use. I lay there and fumed; then I finally got up to make coffee, figuring I could take a nap later in the day. Rafael seemed utterly oblivious.

Though I wanted to yell at him and throw the television out the window, I restrained myself and thought about a rational way to deal with this issue. This was not the first time his actions disturbed me, or his early morning TV watching interrupted my sleep. I had to deal with this as an adult.

Later that day, I asked Rafael if he had a minute to talk; I wanted this to be a conversation and not a confrontation. "I understand you like to watch TV in the morning, but it wakes me up, and sometimes I don't get enough rest. Can we talk about a solution here that meets both our needs?" I asked. He pursed his lips, and I continued. "I know you turn it down low, and I appreciate that, but the light coming from it and the muffled sound keeps me awake..."

Rafael broke in: "Your CPAP makes noise, and I have put up with that without complaining, so you can put up with a little TV."

I paused and then answered, "I don't have a choice with the CPAP." He grew angry and defensive.

"We're supposed to be on vacation! It's the only time I have to watch TV whenever I want!"

I broke in. "OK, maybe we can have a compromise here. What if we say that the television is off until 7 a.m., or another hour that we agree on, so I can get my rest and you can watch TV?" This compromise seemed reasonable to me but not to him.

"I'm not going to tell you that I'm not going to watch TV before 7! I want to watch it whenever I feel like it. You can put up with that like I put up with your CPAP and a lot of other things!" The conversation was escalating; he had no desire to compromise. It was his way or no way. I let the matter drop unresolved since I was dealing with a child.

The following day when he woke up early, he left the room rather than turn on the TV.

There was tension between us, and I wasn't sure how to resolve it. I refused to argue with Rafael about the Jacuzzi incident, and he seemed uninterested in hearing how I felt. When I attempted to sit down and reach a compromise about the television, we were again at a roadblock. I still thought that these were communication issues that we could resolve over time; I was bound by my belief that our relationship was destiny. However, we still had more days in Costa Rica, and I wanted to try to enjoy the remainder with Rafael.

I began to feel much better, so we began to leave the hotel area and go to the local beaches. There was a gay beach nearby which was much easier to get to by car, and Rafael and I went there once, but in the days that followed, he began to go on his own, disappearing for the whole afternoon. I was perplexed by this choice to spend most of the day apart.

A few days later, we ran out of food, so we decided to grab a bite to eat in town, which turned out to be more challenging than we had thought. After exploring a bit, we turned to drive back up the hill. "Let's stop at the market for a minute," I suggested.

"OK," he said as he pulled over.

"Do you want to come in?" I asked.

"No. Now look, I don't want to wait here. Just buy tea and bread, nothing else. Only two minutes." I didn't like being controlled. "I'm just going to look around for a second to see if we need anything else."

Rafael blew up. "No, I'm not going to wait! Just come in and out! If you want to go shopping, do that on your own time!"

I had had enough of this. "I'm going to look around a little, then I'll be right back," I said as I got out of the car. Then Rafael drove off.

I went in to buy some food and expected Rafael to be outside. I thought he might be waiting in the car around the corner, but he wasn't. I began to walk up the hill toward the hotel, which was about a mile away. As I walked, carrying two bags of food for the house, I grew increasingly angry. "This is the last straw!" I said to myself as I made my way in the hot sun. By the time I got near the hotel, I was fuming and wanted to leave Costa Rica immediately. At that moment, a few minutes from the hotel, Rafael drove up and offered me a lift, smiling as if nothing had occurred. Exhausted, I got in but kept silent.

I was too angry to talk when I got back to the hotel. I decided that I would leave this dysfunctional relationship in which I was subject to such abuse. Rafael entered, smiling and joking, but I did not respond. "Are we still going on the Zip Line tour tomorrow?" he asked. I was in no mood for it, but it was paid for already, so I nodded yes. I didn't speak that day, not out of spite or to make him feel bad, but because I wanted to reflect well on my words before I did.

The next day's Zip Line tour was challenging because I was so hurt, upset, and angry. I decided to compartmentalize my feelings and try to have an enjoyable time.

We left the next day for his home in Columbia. The plan was that I would stay with him for five days before returning to California. Since we were on different flights, a friend met me at the airport in his hometown.

On the way to Rafael's house, I opened up about the trip to Enrique, who had known Rafael for many years. Enrique offered a sympathetic ear and expressed his sorrow. He added that he believed Rafael to be an immature person and was not surprised at the course of events.

A few hours later, when Rafael arrived, we sat down to talk. "So how are we?" he asked.

"I can't be in a relationship with someone who treats me the way you do," I said. He began to defend his actions, and I just said, "Enough!"

Then he said, "OK, you are welcome to stay here for the rest of your visit if you want." He then left to go about his things, and I lay down on the bed. I was in turmoil. "Can we call Stefano before making a decision?" Rafael asked. Both Rafael and I had faith in our friendship with Stefano, and he had known both of us for decades.

Rafael got on the phone and spoke with Stefano for a long time. After half an hour, he came into the room and handed me the phone. "Mark, give this more of a chance. You two are so different, but there is love here. Rafael can be difficult, but I have so much hope for you guys. I think you guys can work through this. Rafael is willing to give it a try. Are you?"

If this relationship was going to end, I didn't want it to be a decision born of anger. I wanted to understand what was going on between us; I couldn't let go until it made sense.

I turned to Rafael and said, "Can we try again?" He smiled.

I was feeling hurt, angry, and abused after this trip, yet I needed more evidence or a sign telling me whether I should remain in this relationship or not. I did love and care for Rafael, but what kept me with him was something else. My belief in this relationship as part of my destiny had become a trap.

Part IV: Love and Money in Sicily

I returned home and again volunteered to work the double shift to earn money to be with Rafael. We decided to meet in Sicily because he was moving to

Spain and the flight would be affordable. I offered to pay for the lodging because Rafael earned little. I was fostering a mindset that would soon rear its head.

I arrived in Palermo, where I would meet Rafael. I found a beautiful apartment around the cathedral. It was in a middle-class neighborhood crowded with broken-down buildings, donkeys, and roosters.

I was happy when Rafael arrived; he was amazed by our fantasy apartment, especially the canopy bed. "I need to take a nap," he said as he stripped down and got under the sheets. I got in with him, and we both dozed off.

The cultural sights in Palermo were more incredible than I expected. The churches, museums, and nearby Greek ruins were amazing. Never had I seen so many cultural wonders in the same place. The mentality, however, was unnerving. The following day I spilled coffee granules on the kitchen floor; when we returned that evening, they were still on the floor. The daily visits of the housekeeper consisted of making the bed. Towels went unchanged, and the bathroom was dirty. Only the bed was made.

I loved the cultural heritage in Palermo, but we were ready for the beach area, so we left for the resort town of Taormina. It was perched high on a hill above the beautiful beaches and next to an incredibly preserved Greek theatre.

It was overcast in Taormina when we arrived, so the views were not spectacular, but the town was incredible. We sat and had an overpriced drink at the terrace café where Elizabeth Taylor liked to go (according to my guidebook). We walked down the main street, looking at the shops and their wares, wondering which of them were made in China. The town itself was very touristy but beautiful.

We had not had sex yet during our vacation; it just seemed like the right moment never presented itself. I didn't seek out sexual contact, and neither did Rafael. I figured this was just a stage in the growth of our relationship.

On our second day in Taormina, as Rafael and I were walking down the street, he brought up the subject of his need for a new camera. I said nothing, as he emphasized how useful it would be for his research and teaching, but he could not afford the model he had his eye on, which was over four hundred dollars. He continued to hint, waiting for me to break in and offer to buy it for him, but I didn't. Then he turned to me and said, "If you could find it in yourself to participate in this expense, I would be grateful because I need this." I felt uneasy. My camera cost $100; I couldn't afford an expensive one. I realized that I had created a monster. "I'm not going to do that," I responded. Rafael grew angry.

"I don't think your reasoning is correct on this," he said. "I think you should re-think this decision. We are together, after all, and we should be sharing everything." I thought to myself: "Yeah, but it means you share in all my things, but you give nothing." I stood my ground, and Rafael refused to speak to me the rest of the day. I again found myself with a child.

The next day, Rafael had snapped out of it, and the subject of the camera did not come up again. It was as if nothing had occurred. I was tired of this pattern of behavior.

After a few days, we left Taormina for Catania.

The whole city is made from dark lava rock in a rich baroque style, which I liked, but which the guidebooks described as cold. We had a room at a bed-and-breakfast near the main cathedral, a perfect location. I felt more comfortable in Catania than I had in Palermo.

"I got a recommendation for dinner from the owner of the B&B, and he said they would treat us well if we tell the waiter that he sent us. Let's have a nice calm meal tonight." Rafael agreed.

We asked the waiter to serve us whatever he recommended. He began to bring appetizer after appetizer, types of seafood that I had never seen before, so fresh they could leap off the plate. He recommended a wine, side orders, and the main course, everything swimming in butter. At a certain point, I turned to Rafael and said, "I feel like an Emperor." It was true. We were being given extraordinary service and incredible food in a beautiful location. "I couldn't ask for more," Rafael said contentedly. This meal was one of the highlights of our trip.

We flew up to Rome the next day to conclude our visit with Stefano. The following afternoon we walked up the Capitoline hill to see our rock where we had promised our hearts to each other, but when we arrived, we found that the whole area was walled off due to some type of renovation. Perhaps this was a sign?

Once offered as gifts, the financial help I gave Rafael was now expected. But I had no one to blame but myself. Though I had said that I did not want a partner financially dependent on me, my actions stated the opposite as I took care of one financial need after another. Rafael had learned how to manipulate me; by just dropping hints, he would gain what he desired.

When I finally realized that I had created the situation, he regarded any refusal of help as an insult and rejection. But I was starting to draw boundaries and to see what type of person this Rafael was.

Unsure where this relationship was heading but not yet ready to give up on it, I suggested that we meet in Greece the next time.

Part V: Partners and Friends and in Between

Because of geography, I had not promised monogamy with Rafael when we were apart, but only when we were together. Though he was upset by this arrangement, it was the best that I could offer, though I seldom took advantage of it. But in the months preceding my next planned trip, I reconnected with an acquaintance in Los Angeles from some years back. He was a man with a reputation, and his name was Joshua.

I knew Joshua had never been in a stable relationship in his life, but my direct experience of him was that he was extremely handsome, oozing with charm, and had a caring heart. We met some years before at a grocery store in Los Angeles. We were both in line; he looked at me, and I looked at him. A half-hour later, he was in my bed, and we were having passionate sex. He called the next day when I felt the first signs of a cold coming on. "Do you need anything?" he asked. I reassured him that I was OK. When I became sicker the following day, he would not take "No" for an answer, showing up at my door with cans of soup and juices. I was grateful, but after calling him a few times after I recovered and not hearing back, I let him go.

I asked around about him after this encounter and

was told, "He is a flake," and "Nice guy, but he doesn't keep in touch and is not capable of maintaining a relationship."

Years had passed. It was after my trip to Sicily that he got in touch with me and invited me over. He renovated houses for a living, renting or flipping them, having fifteen or so such properties in Los Angeles.

When I arrived at his place one evening, I was struck by the beauty of both his home and him. When I walked in, he hugged me, and then he kissed me on the lips. "You're even better looking than how I remember you," he said, but I brushed off this compliment.

He invited me to come and sit out on the balcony overlooking Los Angeles. He reached over and held my hand, and I enjoyed the attention of this sexy and charming man. He seemed genuinely interested in my life and asked me many questions about my relationship with Warren and the house. "I have to tell you," I confessed, "I am involved with someone now, Rafael, who lives in Spain." He was not surprised at all.

"That's better because it makes things go slowly." He then got up and led me downstairs to his bedroom.

After another session of passionate sex, we lay in bed and talked. But it was late, and I needed to get home, so I kissed him and said good night.

I wasn't sure if I would see him again, but I was aware of a warm feeling that stayed with me for several days.

I was still committed to Rafael, so I saw this interlude with Joshua as merely sexual. Any talk of something more between us was pure fantasy.

A few days later, I heard from Joshua. "Are we going to get together again soon?" he texted.

"I hope so," was my response. A few days later, we met for dinner. "I feel proud to be seen out with you," he said. After our meal, we shared another evening of kissing and lovemaking.

We continued to see each other several times per week. I loaned him a copy of the book I wrote about my time in a seminary in Rome. A few days later, I heard from him. "I can't put it down! I can't believe how alike we are!" I began to receive very long texts from Joshua about how his search for love paralleled my own. "I am so glad we are connecting on this level," he texted. He was developing feelings for me, but I knew I needed to hold back because I was still with Rafael. I would not get into a situation of pursuing two relationships simultaneously. At least, that is what I told myself.

Rafael was my partner and Joshua a friend. I strove to keep these things separate by not speaking with Joshua about my relationship issues. It was more of a loose "friendship with benefits" arrangement with Joshua with no commitment or obligations. It was simply two men enjoying each other on various levels. What could be wrong with that?

Joshua and I began to text each other many times during the day; we enjoyed checking how the other was doing. The focus of these communications was always on me, however. I knew almost nothing about him except what I heard from others. "Let's talk about you some time," I said one evening when we were in his truck together.

"We'll get to that, but this is all about you right now." I was flattered that he showed such interest in my well-being but still wondered about his secret life.

After some weeks, my feelings began to stir. When

his texts arrived, I started to have an emotional reaction. But I did not pause to reflect on what this meant.

"Can you come over after work to relax in the Jacuzzi with me?" he texted me. Two hours later, we were together.

"Sometimes I come here to pray," he began. "I love the fact that you have faith. God is everything to me. A lot of people don't get that. The fact that we have faith in common means a lot to me, Mark," he continued as he came to my side of the Jacuzzi and put his arm around me. I was attracted to this masculine, sexy man of faith, and I felt more in common with him at that moment than I had with Rafael over the past year. Was this true, or an illusion also?

Over the following days and weeks, Joshua continued to share little of himself, except his childhood. "I had foster parents who abused me," he said in tears one evening. "I can remember spending all day painting the fence around the house, just to get the attention of my foster father. When he came home and saw it, all he did was slap me. I used to imagine myself in Jesus' arms, and that made me feel safe." He seemed unable to free himself from his childhood memories because he brought up this abuse repeatedly. "Have you ever gotten counseling to deal with this?" I asked. "Yes, and it helped. The therapist told me, 'Joshua, it's over. Just hearing him say that helped me to start putting it in my past." But it seemed to me it was very much present.

The only other parts of his life that Joshua spoke about were his high school years. "I was valedictorian in high school, and Prom King, with my girlfriend as Queen. We were in the 'most popular group, and I excelled at my classes, maybe to make up for what was happening at home. I planned to get married to this girl after high school until I realized I might be gay." I knew of his childhood and high school years, but he was silent about his adult life.

As we continued to see each other, I noticed that Joshua was only available on weekdays. "My sister is coming to town," or "My other sister is staying with me." It seemed that his sisters were with him every weekend.

We often had conversations about relationships, and one day I confided in him: "I believe what someone I care about tells me unless I have proof that he is not telling the truth."

"That's just stupid!" was his response.

"Well, I can't live my life in suspicion all the time," I replied. Perhaps his reaction was indicative of the absence of truth in things Joshua told me. I wondered.

We discussed drugs one evening, and I asked him if he used them. "I have, yes. Does that bother you?"

"I lost Warren to Crystal, and I will not go through that again."

Joshua looked at me. "I would never put you through that, honey. I haven't used in over a year. And I am making a decision now not to use again," he said as he got up and rummaged through his closet. Out of a briefcase, he pulled out three small bags of Crystal Meth. He walked to the bathroom. "I hope you are doing this for you and not for me," I called out. He dumped them in the toilet and flushed.

"I am doing it for me. I shouldn't be screwing with my body anyway," he said as he got into bed. "Can you stay with me tonight? Please?" he asked. "Yes, but not tonight because I need my CPAP machine. But I will," I promised.

We began sleeping together that following week, and it was a refreshing experience to stay with such a seemingly caring man.

"I've got to go to the gym, but I'll be back by 7," he whispered in my ear. It was 5 a.m. "Please stay and wait for me." I nodded and dozed off as he kissed me on the cheek. I was developing feelings for this man, though my denial was growing in equal proportion.

I had a reality check late one morning after I got home when Rafael called. "Where were you last night?" he asked.

"What are you talking about?" I answered.

"I called and called, but no answer," he replied.

"I turned off the phone to sleep late. I missed your call. But here I am. How are you?" I could tell he wanted to quiz me further, but I wouldn't allow that. He was in Spain, and I was in California. Was he going to try to control me even from there?

My friend Thomas had met Joshua years before, so we all decided to meet for lunch. It was a workday, but I had an extended lunch period. "Why don't I pick you up from school, so you don't lose your parking space?" Joshua offered. A few hours later, I got into his truck, and we made our way to a favorite Japanese, hole-in-the-wall restaurant. The three of us had a satisfying meal and light conversation; after half an hour, I was on my way back to school. When we pulled in front of my building, Joshua said, "A good friend of mine is a psychic, and I told her about you. She said that you are special; you are not like anyone else I have been with. She hopes I don't lose you. Damn, I hope I don't screw this one up!" I took his hand, squeezed it, and got out.

Joshua had lots of properties and was, in real estate value, a millionaire. I was never clear, however, how he got this money in the first place. He owned a cabin in the mountains and asked me to accompany him there a few weeks later. "My men are working on it, and I want to check it and show it to you," he said. We set off and arrived a few hours later. "You are the first one seeing this, and you will be the first who sleeps here," he said as we pulled up. It was a beautiful A-frame cabin that he was remodeling. It was surrounded by pine trees and situated in a peaceful setting.

"What do you think, Mark?" Joshua asked.

"I love it," I said.

"I would love to just move up here with you, have a simple life, raise Akitas (his favorite dog breed), and just be happy together," he said with a smile. I was being drawn in by this fantasy.

Something was growing between us, though it was not defined. "I'm glad we are building a firm foundation here," Joshua said one day. "We're moving nice and slow, and that's what I want so that what we have will last." It sounded like a pledge of permanency.

I only knew the Joshua that I experienced, who was full of charm, interested in me, extremely considerate, and loving. But there were unanswered questions also: Why was he always unavailable on weekends? Who were his friends, and why had I not met them? What about his reputation as a flake and someone who could not be relied upon? Was he trying to turn over a new leaf and find some stability with one person?

Other questions began to emerge about myself: Why was I developing feelings for Joshua? What was missing in my relationship with Rafael that I was trying to fill with this almost stranger?

I had planned a trip to Rome and Greece during my vacation days to spend time with Rafael; this would give me some perspective on the situation with Joshua. I was looking forward to this vacation and wanted to be open to what it might bring.

Part VI: Growing Apart in Athens

As had happened many times in the past, I came down with a cold a few days before my departure. The plan was to meet Rafael in Rome, stay a few days in an apartment in Trastevere, and continue to Athens. I hoped that I could recover in Rome and be ready for our Greek adventure.

Though pleased to see Rafael, the overwhelming joy I felt in the past was absent. I was guided by the belief that love makes two people compatible. The differences between the two personalities would be smoothed out by the sheer affection they have for the other. This trip would prove whether this belief held.

Our lodging was a small studio in an excellent location. I went to find some food items and, though it was hot, brewed hot tea to clear my sinuses. I sipped it, and Rafael and I shared about our flights and what we were looking forward to in Greece. "I'm tired," he said as he lay down, and I decided to rest, too. It was already late in the afternoon.

Rafael was energetic the following day, but I was still fighting my cold. We decided to explore our neighborhood and get breakfast. "What do you feel like doing this afternoon?" he asked.

"I'll probably stay close to home in case I don't feel

well, maybe explore the neighborhood. Why?"

He responded, "I think I'll take a walk around, maybe stop at the sauna to look. You are going to rest anyway, so what am I supposed to do? Just sit there?" I didn't object. The day after I arrived, Rafael headed over to the bathhouse.

As I was lying in bed, I became restless. I was not so ill that I needed to stay inside, so I went out and took a walk in Trastevere. Rafael had left hours ago, and I began feeling hurt and irritated. Though I had my fling back in Los Angeles, this seemed different. We were together at a great financial sacrifice, and he was at a bathhouse. I would never tell him what he should or should not do because I wanted the desire to be together to come from him. But I wondered, as the day passed and I grew agitated, just what I meant to him. It was close to 8 p.m. when he returned home, telling me that there was no one attractive at the bathhouse, that it was a waste of time, etc. His usual story. I shook my head but said nothing.

Later that evening, we headed out and had a pleasant dinner.

In the preceding weeks, I had told Rafael about my friendship with Joshua but left out the part about the sex and emotional stirrings. Perhaps he suspected something. When I left my cell phone unattended the next day, he opened the email and read the correspondence between Joshua and me. Though he knew little English, he confronted me. "What is this?" he asked angrily. I repeated that Joshua was a friend.

"It doesn't sound like just a friend from the emails between you two!" he said.

"You read my email? You had no right to do that!"

I countered. He brushed that off and began to grill me. "He is a friend, and that is all. I have no more to say," I repeated. He grew angry but eventually let it go. I felt violated. I wondered how this trip would go because we were just in our first days of three weeks together, and already I wished I was alone.

I figured that once we arrived in Greece, we would be swept up in the cultural marvels and be less focused on each other and our issues.

A few days later, arriving in Greece, Athens' dinginess was more than outweighed by the Acropolis and the museums. It was a history buff's banquet. Rafael and I got along well when it came to seeing the cultural sights, but within a few hours after arriving at our apartment, he was on the computer seeking out the location of the nearest bathhouses. "I'm going to go and explore the gay scene," he announced. I thought the situation was getting ridiculous but said nothing, knowing that only an argument would ensue.

I was making tea that evening when Rafael returned because I was still not well. "How was it?" I asked.

"It took me a long time to find it, and it was empty. I sat in the Jacuzzi and the steam room, then I left," he said.

"Was it worth it?" I asked. He shook his head.

After dinner, we decided to get to bed early because we would spend the following day at the archeological museum. But I still had jet lag. I awoke in the middle of the night and got up to read in the living room. After a while, I picked up my cell phone to check my email and found a short message from Joshua. I wrote out a response, describing what I had seen so far. "Mark, what are you doing?" Rafael called out.

"Reading, I'll be there in a minute," I answered. I completed the email and returned to bed to try to sleep.

The museum was incredible and exhausting because there were so many beautiful things to see.

After our museum visit, we got a bite to eat and returned to the apartment to rest in the afternoon. As I sat down with a cup of tea, Rafael sat next to me and said, "You lied to me." I looked at him, bewildered. "Last night, you got up. I could see you through the curtains. I asked you what you were doing, and you said you were reading. But I could see you, typing away on your phone. Was it to this Joshua again?" I felt angry and overly controlled by him. "I read a while, answered some email, and came to bed." I refused to answer any more of his questions. Then I lay down to rest, but I was too irritated to fall asleep.

The event passed without being further discussed, and we managed to have a beautiful evening walking up the Acropolis hill at night. When we made our way down, we heard music and walked to that side of the hill. There was a full orchestra practicing for a concert the following evening. As we stopped to listen, the notes carried through the ruins of ancient Athens.

I found a tourist office the next day. We decided to investigate whether we could afford a bus tour to Delphi and Meteora. We walked up the dingy stairs and found ourselves in a waiting area. I turned to Rafael to ask him his preferences for the tour when I noticed, looking square at him, that he now had a diamond earring in one ear. I was surprised and dismayed because it represented to me how distant we had become. After leaving the office, when he saw me looking at his ear, he asked me if I liked it. "No, I don't," I said.

The next day, on the tour bus, Rafael mostly slept or listened to his iPod while I gazed out the window at the changing Greek countryside. I was tired when we pulled up to the hotel, then dismayed when the announcement came that this was not our lodging. There were several drop-offs, and ours was the last one. Rafael took off his earphones and looked out the window. "Mark, they are removing suitcases. Go make sure they don't take yours by mistake," he said. I shook my head. "They are all labeled; it will be fine," and I sank back into my seat.

When we did exit our bus at our hotel some twenty minutes later, my suitcase was missing. "It must be at the first hotel," the tour guide said. "Don't worry, the driver will go and get it right now; it's not a problem." I was irritated, but when I turned to Rafael, he was furious, not at the situation, but me. "I told you to get off the bus and check your suitcase! You're so hard-headed; you never listen to anyone!" he began.

I walked away as he spoke. When he approached me again, I said, "I'll handle this. You can go to the room and relax." He wanted to argue, and I didn't, so this infuriated him more. I refused to be the brunt of his abuse when I was already concerned about my suitcase. He left and went to the room, and my bag arrived a few minutes later.

I went upstairs; Rafael was moping, but I refused to get tangled up in this. "Look, we are here, in a beautiful hotel, a nice area, a pool. Can we get past this and not devote time to stress?" I asked. He nodded, so we changed and went swimming.

We took a walk that evening, and the next day toured the nearby monasteries, which were a marvel.

Most of them are not functioning anymore, with a token monk in a strategic location for tourists. They were like shells, but I am glad I was able to experience them. We then took the long bus ride back to Athens.

I enjoyed our visit to mainland Greece. The art, history, and archeology were amazing, but I did not feel happy with Rafael. I felt controlled, criticized, and abandoned. The promise of happiness that I experienced with him that first day we met in Rome was not being fulfilled. It was clear that between Rafael and me, there was a space, like a fog that separated us increasingly, but neither was ready to address.

The love between us had not overcome our differences, and our lack of compatibility was making each of us increasingly irritated with each other. My belief that love would overcome these differences had not held.

Part VII: Mykonos and Love's Illusions

We had a day of rest before we proceeded on the next part of our trip. I was excited as we boarded the ferry for Mykonos; we found excellent seats with a table.

I felt detached from Rafael on board and wondered about what this leg of the trip would bring.

When we pulled up to Mykonos, a muscle-bound police officer was waiting at the dock. "I think we are in the right place," Rafael said. We then made our way to the town, where we found our apartment on the outskirts. I had obtained a reasonable rate because it was off-season.

The point of going to Mykonos was to go to the

beaches, and I suggested that we walk into town to see what transportation was available.

"We should just rent a car," Rafael stated.

"I think we should first see whether there are busses or vans that go out there to save money." He became irate. It seemed his anger was flaring up at me every day, and I was tired of this.

"I want to rent the car now!" he demanded. This was the exact disagreement that we had in Costa Rica.

I was on the defense. "I'm going out for a few hours," I stated.

He looked up and asked, "Can you wait for me? I want to go out, too." I reluctantly agreed and, after a few minutes, he was ready. As we walked toward the center of town, we said nothing to each other. I could feel the tension and anger. We were silent as he walked into a shop while I waited outside. Minutes passed, so I slowly began to continue walking, often looking back so he could catch up. But he remained in the store. I continued to walk. I needed some space; I needed to cool off and think. I explored the town on my own and eventually found the bus depot, where I asked about transportation to the beaches. I discovered that busses were crowded and infrequent, so perhaps renting the car would be a good decision.

I was not yet ready to return to the apartment and deal with Rafael, so I followed signs in the town to an internet café where I checked my email. I found a message from Joshua. I had never divulged to him the problems in my relationship with Rafael, but here in Mykonos, I filled him in. I was upset, so it was a way to vent my feelings. When he responded to my email right away, we both discovered that we were both online at the exact moment, so we wrote back and forth, me complaining about Rafael's anger and Joshua consoling me.

I felt uneasy about sharing these things with Joshua because I had not used him as a relationship confidant. Keeping my rapport with Rafael and Joshua separate seemed to be the best thing. These two relationships were intertwined as I told him what happened in Rome, in Athens, and now in Mykonos. "You don't deserve that, Mark. I am so happy to hear from you, though. I feel like I am with you right now!" he wrote. Having unloaded my heart, I felt better. I was now ready to deal with Rafael.

When I walked into the room, the first thing that Rafael said accusingly was, "You said you were only going to be away for a few hours!"

I responded that I just needed some time. Then, to cut off this line of conversation, I asked, "Do you want to go rent this car now?" He jumped up, and we rented the car.

We found out where the gay beach was and headed out there the next day. Though off-season, the place was crowded with men of all sizes, all with tiny bathing suits. We found a spot under an umbrella, and Rafael and I lay down. I had brought a book and spent time reading, going into the water, exploring the beach, and watching the crowds. Rafael and I took turns, one of us staying to guard our belongings while the other roamed or swam. "I wonder what is over those rocks there," I said when he returned. I climbed up the rocky hill and down the other side, where I found a few secluded beaches where the men were wearing no bathing suits at all. I was curious, so I walked up and down the beach and rocks, looking at men sunning themselves, swimming, and some cruising for sex.

Rafael and I had not had sex at all this trip, and I felt little sexual desire.

I came back to our umbrella and told Rafael what I had seen. He immediately hopped up and climbed the same rocks. Hours passed in this way, as we took turns under the umbrella, walking, looking, swimming, and resting.

On one of my excursions, I noticed a Greek man staring at me in the nude section. He was moderately handsome, masculine, dark-skinned, had a beard and a nice body. He got up and began to follow me. I was more curious than anything else, so I walked back to a secluded area. As I turned, he pushed down his bathing suit and reached inside of mine. Before I knew it, I was engaged in a sexual encounter that was fun and frightening at the same time. The whole thing lasted no more than ten minutes. I quickly said my goodbyes and went into the water to wash off any evidence of sex. Now I felt scared; what if Rafael had been walking by and had seen? What if he asked me what happened? What if he found some evidence? I stayed and washed even longer.

In the water, my mind went in all directions. I had been telling myself that I had not had sex with Rafael because I had not been feeling sexual, and yet with this stranger, my physical response was immediate. Perhaps there was more to the lack of sex between us than I had been admitting to myself?

I sheepishly made my way back to our umbrella, where I found Rafael sleeping. I was relieved, laid down, put my hat over my face, and attempted to rest.

He didn't know what happened, but I had much to reflect on.

After dinner, we found ourselves in a club where a live show was about to begin. A young American woman was preparing to sing with a pianist. We looked around and saw that almost all of the seats were already taken. A waiter spotted us and guided us further in until we ended up sitting right in front of the stage. When she began singing "Both Sides Now" by Joni Mitchell, tears came to my eyes. Though she sang a sugary version, the words cut me to the core. The feelings of love becoming an illusion rang true as I thought of these days, months, and years with Rafael. What had seemed so genuine now felt so empty. When we left, I was sad.

"Mark, I'm going to stay out and see what these other bars are like. I met some guys from Spain who I'm going to look for," Rafael said as we were making our way home. Though I was glad to have some time to myself, his choice to spend the evening separate seemed to confirm the song's words.

The following day, Rafael expressed the desire to go to Paradise beach on his own. Though he complained of us having separate vacations, I saw this as his choice. I suggested we meet up in the afternoon. He again seemed irritated at me, so I was grateful to again have some time to myself.

Unanswered questions and tensions were bubbling to the surface in Mykonos. I felt uneasy, unhappy, and unvalued. Something had to change, and I was ready to abandon my belief that my relationship with Rafael was meant to be.

Part VIII: Santorini: Wanting Out

After four nights in Mykonos, we had another four in Santorini before returning to Athens then Rome. Santorini, I had been told, was one of the most beautiful places in the world, and I looked forward to our arrival. It was not a gay destination, so I hoped for less tension with Rafael.

Santorini rests on an underwater volcano that exploded, and part of the cone remains above the water. The highlights of the island are the sunsets, which no words can describe. Our apartment was located about fifty yards from a ledge where there was a breathtaking view of the sea. We were happy with our lodgings and decided to explore.

We soon discovered that the town of Fira, the capital where we were staying, was tiny. It consisted of a long pedestrian road along the ledge and a parallel route for cars further down. Lined with restaurants and shops, it was a tourist trap. Though beautiful, we realized that there was not much to do in town but shop.

We decided to explore beyond the town. We took a boat trip to an island where the ground itself was hot to the touch due to volcanic activity; we also went to the other side of the island to watch a sunset that was so beautiful that the onlookers clapped as the sun dipped behind the horizon. Rafael was restless and seemed bored. I figured he missed the gay life of Mykonos.

The next day, as the sun was beginning to set, we found a beautiful place from which to enjoy it, sitting at a table on a ledge over the sea, with two glasses of wine and some appetizers. It seemed like the most fantastic spot in the world. Everything was perfect and serene until Rafael asked me a question.

"What do you think of our relationship? How are we doing?"

I paused as I thought of the most honest answer that I could give him at that moment. "I don't know," I replied.

"What do you mean, you don't know? Are you unsure of us?"

"I am unsure of us and our future," was my response.

These words unleashed Rafael's fury. "How could you say such a thing? You're incredible! After all this time, you are unsure? I can't share my life with someone who is so uncertain. I want to leave! I want to go! I want to get out of here! I want to go back to Rome, back to Spain! I don't want to be with someone like this. Are you unsure? That means you don't want this relationship, but you can't say it! I don't want this. You will never decide what you want! You will be alone! This is absurd!" and he continued in this vein for some time. He then rose from the table and said, "I'm leaving Santorini. I don't like it here, I'm going to leave," and with that, he left the restaurant.

I sat at the table, stunned. But I soon became aware of a peculiar feeling that I had not experienced in an awfully long time. It was subtle, and I could barely perceive it, barely touch it. But it was there, at the bottom of my heart. It took a while to find the word for it: relief.

I found an internet café and drafted long emails to some of my friends, reaching out for emotional support. One of my friends, Brandon, wrote back immediately. "Well, maybe God is doing for you what you could not do for yourself." His words confirmed my feelings.

I didn't want to deal with Rafael, so I avoided the apartment. I didn't want to argue, talk, feel bad, or be the object of his anger. If he was going to leave the island, then let him leave.

I remembered a monastery I saw and made my way up the hill and found the church unlocked. I went in and knelt. It was evening.

I asked God to guide me through these events to a better place, towards the other peaceful shore of this river of troubles, and help me be open. I also prayed that Rafael might find his way.

When the church closed, I took my time in finding something to eat. It was nearly 10 p.m., and I ran out of things to do, so I headed home. I figured that Rafael would be gone, and I could breathe deeply, but when I entered the apartment, he was in his bed, and all his things were packed. He had pushed his bed to the other side of the room. I figured he must have a morning flight, so I quietly took off my clothes and slipped under my sheets.

He got up early the following day. I pretended I was asleep until he left the room. His luggage was still there, so I was not yet in the clear. But I made myself a coffee, took a shower, dressed, and headed toward the monastery. When I left the room, however, Rafael was sitting outside, at a table, reading. He didn't look up or say hello, so I turned and walked away.

The monastery was a place of peace, but I was still in turmoil and uncomfortable. I was ready to leave the relationship and grateful that I did not have to make the first move. But I also felt much pain and wanted the separation to be over.

I left the monastery for the internet café to check for other responses to my emails because I was searching for support. I found several long messages from friends who encouraged me not to forget that this trip was for me and to enjoy myself even if Rafael left. They also pointed out to me a pattern in Rafael's behavior that had been going on for years. Time to move on, my friends said.

I wanted to avoid drama, so I avoided the apartment, hoping that Rafael would depart while I was out.

Having eaten lunch, I returned to the monastery, but I grew tired and wanted to rest. I would have to take a chance of seeing Rafael at the apartment, but likely, he was already gone. I made my way back but was dismayed when I found Rafael there. He didn't speak to me, so I lay down and shut my eyes.

I didn't want to argue, I didn't want to discuss, and I wanted no stress. I longed for this to be over.

Rafael lay down on his bed, but I kept my eyes shut. I would rest a bit, I thought, and then return to town and the monastery later. This was my plan as Rafael spoke, "Mark, can we talk?" I groaned interiorly. "Yes," I said as I opened my eyes.

We talked for several hours, Rafael doing most of the talking and me the listening. He repeated how much he loved me. At one point, tears rolled down his cheeks. "I always arrive too late. It is as if I arrived too late in your life," he said as he wept.

I was hoping not to have to discuss these things. I wanted this to be over. I especially did not want to backtrack because the decision to break up was his, and I was good with that. But he continued. "I love you so much, and I don't want to lose you! I know I am immature; I know that. But I was hoping you would be patient with me." He began to cry again. "You should go. You would be better without me. I cannot give you what you need. I'm in Spain; you are in California. I can't give you that life that you want. You should go," and he wept and wept.

My rescuing side was kicking in, so I held him as he cried.

As I listened to Rafael and held him, he calmed down. We didn't resolve anything, but he seemed to feel better after the emotional venting. "Are we OK now?" he asked.

Though my mouth said, "Yes," my heart said, "Damn! It's going to be on me to leave him now!"

We both had enough of Santorini and its memories, so we went to the airport that day to change our tickets for an early departure to Rome.

Because Rafael had some academic affairs to attend to in Rome, I had free time to reflect on this trip. I made a conscious decision to enjoy this last part of my vacation and wait until I got home to decide. Rafael, for his part, seemed to have bounced back to his old self, just like he always had.

I was relieved when I boarded the plane. I felt emotionally safe, which I didn't feel when I was with him these past weeks.

Part IX: Decision Time

Once home, it became clear that I needed to leave this relationship. Because Rafael's birthday was coming up, I decided to postpone communicating this decision until afterward.

This was my mindset until Rafael called me one day. "Mark, I have the opportunity to come to stay with you over Christmas vacation. But I must book the ticket now. Will that work for you?" he asked. I figured I could stall.

"Let me check the dates and get back to you." He was insistent, but I had to be also because I didn't want him planning a trip while I was planning a breakup.

I went to Florida to spend a few days with my friend Phillip, and inevitably the conversation turned to the men in my life. Ever his blunt self, Phillip said, "Rafael is bad news for you. You should have been out of that relationship years ago. As far as this Joshua, I have heard of him. His reputation stretches to Florida. He gets people to fall in love with him, and then he drops them, causing lots of destruction in peoples' lives. It's a game he plays. Be careful, Mark."

When I arrived back in Los Angeles, Rafael started calling me to schedule his Los Angeles trip. His birthday was past, so I needed to act. I put my decision in writing: a simple email stating that I was stepping out of our relationship, and we could speak further about it when he was ready. I got no response. The relationship was over; I regretted how I communicated the break up with him and the hurt that I must have caused Rafael. But I did not want to risk allowing myself to be talked out of the breakup. It was there, in black and white: our relationship was no longer working for me. It's time for both of us to step back and begin to heal. Once the email was sent, I again sensed that subtle feeling of relief that I had felt in Santorini: relief.

Part X: Lessons about Compatibility

Though I entered a relationship with Rafael in the belief that there was some sort of divine plan that indicated we were supposed to be partners, the differences between us contradicted this. The insight that I gained through him, that I could have a happy life due to my choices, remained true. What was not true was that this happiness consisted of being in a relationship with Rafael. It took time and experiences for me to be able to distinguish these.

The problem with the belief that I am "meant" to be with someone after having a strong emotional or sexual experience is that this belief can become an obstacle in getting to know the other person for who he/she is. Different habits, interests, and personalities become swept under the carpet of destiny. A leap of faith is taken. It is like stepping from an extraordinary beginning to a complete commitment while skipping the phase of getting to know each other. Committing without knowing each other can cause surprise, disappointment, and regret.

Though I no longer held that I was meant to be with Rafael, I did believe that he came into my life at the right time. He gave me a gift by helping me see that I had the choice to stay in an addictive relationship or not. I no longer had to see myself as essential to somebody's happiness, only to my own. I no longer had to spend all my energy ensuring that those I cared about were all right. I could focus on building a relationship with myself. By meeting Rafael, I realized that a relationship or person wasn't my destiny. No, happiness was my destiny.

Financial boundaries make for a healthier relationship. If someone had told me this at the beginning of my relationship with Rafael, I would have stared as if they were speaking an alien language. Love was sharing in all aspects of each other's lives, I thought. But this was enmeshment and not love. The signal that something was wrong with this was that Rafael expected me to take care of his financial needs and became irate when I did not. I had created this expectation that was the fruit of my actions. I had to re-think this belief and decided that it no longer served me. Without a clear understanding between the two parties, financial dependence can sow seeds of expectations and resentments, which I saw bloom in my relationship with Rafael.

I carried over my belief that love is enough to make two people compatible from a previous relationship. Though Rafael and I had parallel life experiences in our education and the time we spent in Rome, I eventually could not ignore many personality, temperament, and expectation differences. My belief that love would solve all differences proved to be an obstacle to an accurate assessment of our relationship and prevented me from asking myself whether this was the type of relationship or man I wanted. The belief that love would fill in incompatibility gaps proved to be untrue because, ultimately, Rafael and I did not want the same thing. What I had in mind as a satisfying, loving, and fulfilling relationship was quite different from his vision; we were not, therefore, working toward the same goal. Eventually, this became clear as we became increasingly alienated from each other during our time together in various parts of the world.

The passion of the first love would eventually diminish; the overwhelming emotion that made all challenges easy would lessen, and the joy of being together would become a pattern or routine. When this happens, what is there left to hold two people together? A more genuine love starts here, right where the everydayness sets in.

The last word on this relationship with Rafael is gratitude that he showed me that I had choices, that happiness could be my lot also, and that I didn't have to wait for someone to change to have a fulfilling life.

Chapter 5: Believing He Changed

Things do not change; we change.
Henry David Thoreau

Beliefs:
This time it will be different for me.
I can have a sexual relationship without growing emotionally attached.

Part I: Patterns Destined to Repeat

Though I no longer had Rafael in my life, Joshua was still present. I was unsure of what role he would play.

In the days after my breakup with Rafael, I became aware that Joshua became more distant. Whereas before he was texting me six or seven times a day, now it was once. When I shared anything personal, he threw it back on me as a criticism.

After several days of this, I sent Joshua a text: "Is there something wrong between us that I don't know about?"

I waited for a response, which came a few hours later. "Can I drop by your place this afternoon?"

Joshua showed up later with his dog. He sat down and began, "Mark, I am breaking this off between us. I don't feel safe with you. The fact that you had allowed Warren to mistreat you in the past makes me feel that you could allow someone to take advantage of me. If I were you, I would have hit Warren. You're like this gentle giant. I guess I have more testosterone than you!"

I didn't understand. "Are you saying that you cannot see me anymore because, when I was with Warren, I didn't slug him?"

He shook his head. "You're twisting my words. I was abused as a child. I can't be with someone I don't feel safe with." I was also perplexed and wondered if I was misunderstanding what he was saying.

"Can we sit outside together?" he asked. We went out on the balcony, and he took my hand. I waited for further explanation. But after a few minutes, he said, "I have to go," and got up and left.

I had a delayed reaction to the whole encounter with Joshua. I went to my sister's house that evening and took a walk to think. Joshua broke off our rapport, claiming that the reason was that he was more of a man than I was because he would have struck Warren rather than taking the steps that I did. What didn't add up here?

The more I thought about it, the angry angrier I became. Joshua did what he always does: he cultivated an emotional connection until I developed feelings for him, and then he cut it off. The end of my relationship with Rafael was the end for him also. What angered me was placing the blame on my shoulders, claiming that something was wrong with me. I was also angry with myself for believing that he was different from who he had been in the past.

In the days following, I realized how attached to Joshua I had become. What had started as an acquaintance had evolved into a friendship with benefits, leading to a full-blown emotional bond. I now knew this because I was plunged into sadness. But why? Why had he done this? What were his intentions from the beginning? Why didn't I listen when I had been warned about him?

These questions and others bounced around in my head, and I began to look for answers. Asking around about him, I discovered that everybody in the gay community in Los Angeles knew Joshua. They had either slept with him, had been hurt by him, or had heard about him. "He has a terrible reputation in Los Angeles," a friend of mine from the gym, Rick, told me one day. "He has damaged people. He hurt his ex, Ethan, who was renting an apartment from Joshua. When Ethan left town for a few days, he found all his furniture and belongings gone on his return. Joshua had emptied them and put them into storage to get Ethan out of his life. I knew Ethan; when I bumped into him a few days later and asked him about Joshua, he said that he was an "emotional vampire" and that everything he said about himself was a lie.

I was curious about some of the stories that Joshua had told me, so I asked Ethan about Joshua's high school years, his story about being valedictorian and popular at school, having a girlfriend, etc. "The truth is," Ethan said, "he dropped out of high school and had to finish later. He never went to college. Did you know he has a partner? I think their relationship is non-sexual, but they have been together for years. But they do not live together." I thought having some of my questions answered would resolve this for me. Instead, this information fed my anger as I became aware that I had been used.

"Joshua is the most hated man in the gay community in Los Angeles!" a therapist friend of mine told me one day. "He flew out of Fresno with only his good looks and latched on to the first older wealthy man he could find. He lived as a 'kept man.' I can tell you the names of the men he has lived off. How do you think he got all the money he has? He uses other people. He has a taste for older, wealthy men. That may have changed, however, because he is a wealthy man himself. Now he is just after the emotional high."

I wanted to confront Joshua with this information. Did he have a partner? Were his stories about his past all lies? Was all this just a game to him? I wanted to make him face himself, make him admit that he continued the pattern with me that he had begun many years before with others. After a month had passed with no word from him, I sent him a text. "I'd like to see you when you have time." I wanted a confrontation.

"Mark, you need to get past this," my friend Nathan told me. "If talking with him will help get this in your past, or writing to him, or whatever you need to do, do it. This connection with this guy is bad for you. It's time to move on."

I thought about his words. When I received a text back from Joshua saying that he would have some time the following week, I wondered whether I already had the answers that I sought and if waiting for this meeting would only prolong my anxiety. But I could not let go until I had my final word. But as the days passed, I realized that I needed to wrap up this situation without waiting another week. I sat down and wrote him an email. I felt that I needed to frame what happened in terms that were more accurate than Joshua's reading of things without expressing anger. Then I could let it go

Dear Joshua,

I have found myself anxious about what I want to say when I see you, so perhaps it is simply better that I say it through an email and be done with it. When our relationship ended, I was hurt and angry. Upon reflection, I concluded that the end of the relationship was the repetition of a pattern. When the other person becomes vulnerable and develops feelings, you drop him.

This made me feel like merely one in a series, calling into question any intimate moment or connection that I had thought was real.

But then I had to realize my part. I knew this history, so I had no right to expect that things would be different with me from previous romantic connections.

My anger at you dissipated as I realized that you are very consistent in relationships. I was angry at myself then for moving from friendship to a more profound attachment while ignoring this history. But I had to also forgive myself and move forward.

I wish you happiness.

About an hour later, he wrote back; it was a mean and angry email. He rejected everything I wrote and insulted me from beginning to end. I felt relieved, however. It was over. It was done. I could walk away.

Part II: Lessons about Emotions and Sex

Though Joshua had an established pattern and reputation for using others for his emotional high, I believed it would be different with me this time around. I had no grounds for this belief outside of Joshua's charm. Still, my increasing alienation from Rafael made Joshua's expressions of concern and affection sound like a symphony to my ears. But when the relationship with Rafael ended and I suddenly became dateable, the game was over.

The learning experience was the destruction of my belief that past patterns somehow do not predict future behavior. My feelings were hurt, and I was sad, but I had set this situation up and put myself in front of the boulder that would inevitably roll down the hill. It did roll, I was struck, and though I wanted to blame the boulder, I had to look at what choices and events had put me in its path.

I had not intended to become emotionally attached to Joshua. We were acquaintances, becoming friends, and were having sex. People did this all the time: "friends with benefits." You both get your needs taken care of within a safe environment. I believed that I could separate sex from love, but the experience with Joshua revealed that I could not. An ongoing sexual relationship for me would lead to an emotional attachment that could make my life complicated. Though others could separate the two, I had to admit, after the Joshua affair, that I could not. I would not be able to mix sex and friendship again if I wanted to keep my emotional life stable.

Though the affair with Joshua was of short duration, I'm grateful for the important lessons that it imparted. I deserved and longed for the respect that was lacking in my relationship with Rafael; the brief relationship with Joshua revealed this longing. I am grateful for understanding that the best predictor of future behavior is someone's past patterns. I had to take responsibility for the knowledge I had of Joshua before getting involved. Setting healthy boundaries and separating sex from friendship to preserve a stable emotional life was the most important lesson that I derived from this experience. For this, I am grateful.

Chapter 6: Friendships that Endure

Love does not consist of gazing at each other but in looking outward together in the same direction.
Antoine de Saint-Exupéry

Beliefs:

Friends can become family.

Friendship must be nurtured with time and energy.

Part I: Awkward Beginnings

Thomas had been my best friend for over twenty years, and our friendship continued through all my explorations of love. However, I had few other friends in Los Angeles because I had been keeping myself busy with relationships. I realized that this was unhealthy and decided that I would reach out to develop some new friendships. I believed that intimacy without sex was possible in the gay world.

My first attempts to make new friends were sometimes awkward, and those I contacted were not always sincere. Initially, I reached out over websites. "Would you like to grab a coffee at Starbucks? I am only looking for friendship," was the message I sent to a man named Greg.

"Yes, let's meet. See if you like what you see," was

the response.

I sent another message to clarify: "I'm not looking for sex or a date, only for friends. Let me know if you are interested." Greg replied in agreement, so we planned on meeting the next day, which was a frigid day for Los Angeles.

"Mark, I have a runny nose, so I am not sure I can make it today," Greg texted me a few hours before our appointment. I texted back that I was heading there anyway; he could either come or not come; it was up to him. As I got closer to the coffee house, Greg texted that he would meet me there.

I sat down with my warm coffee on a very chilly day. I was facing away from the window when something caught my eye. I turned around to see a tall, somewhat muscular man, wearing a skimpy tank top, making his way toward Starbucks. "I hope not," I said to myself. It turned out to be him.

He seemed dressed for sex, not friendship. I rose and greeted Greg and offered him a chair. "I'm going to go order coffee," he said as he got in line. I already felt uncomfortable.

When he returned, Greg sat next to me, so close that occasionally his leg touched mine. "How long have you been in Los Angeles?" I asked as I studied his face. It was clear that Greg had some work done, which was confirmed when he lifted the coffee to his lips, which protruded like a fish, and began to suck the coffee up through the hole in the lid. There was something unnatural about his lips and eyes. I realized I was staring, so I looked away.

"I've been here for years, and I am finding that it takes time to make friends," I explained. I told him

194

a bit about my history and what I sought, but there was no chemistry here. He was looking for something else, and I began to feel more uncomfortable as his leg pressed against mine again. When he got up to go to the bathroom, I paused to figure out what to do. When he returned, I excused myself, explaining that I received a call, and thanked him for his time. Greg urged me to phone him when I was free. Five minutes later, I was driving home.

When I bumped into Greg some weeks later, I said hello. His response was to give me a dirty look and turn around. I was grateful that I never let such a person into my life.

Part II: Seeds Planted

Other encounters were more successful. Reed from West Hollywood was personable, intelligent, and felt his emotions deeply. He struck me as a man of integrity as we got to know each other over coffee at the same Starbucks. "This is like an interview room," I said jokingly. When I walked back to my car, and Reed invited me to come up to his place, I declined, telling him I needed to get to work early the next day. I wanted to make sure that this started and continued as a friendship, leaving sex out of it. Reed sent me a message later, saying that he looked forward to when we could get together again. "Me too. I want something more lasting than just a hook-up." Our friendship continued to grow in affection and mutual respect.

My first meeting with Juan (not Juan Luis, another Juan), some weeks later, was sexual. We enjoyed ourselves so much that we got together again, and it was then that I realized that there was much more to Juan than a hot Latin man. He had substance, integrity, and a good heart: a true man. This was a quality person that I wanted to keep in my life.

Not limited by his profession as an architect, Juan pursued his passion for history by volunteering at a local museum. He was a pilot and flew a small plane on weekends; he was also knowledgeable about science and movies, and jazz music. He was a renaissance man.

Juan had been married and had children and grandchildren, as well as an ex-wife with whom he was on good terms. He had raised his family and was dipping his toe into gay life when we met. His rich experience, big heart, and passion for knowledge intrigued me.

Over the following weeks and months, my friendship with Juan blossomed. He was fascinated by the fact that I practiced my faith. "If I walk into a church, I'll be struck by lightning!" he remarked. A few weeks later, his attitude changed, and he met me at a gay-friendly church in West Hollywood. It became our weekly ritual to meet at Starbucks before the service, attend church together, and then meet other friends for brunch.

Over time the contact between Juan and me grew in depth; it reached the point at which, if the one had not heard from the other after a few hours, inevitably a text would arrive: "You OK, baby?" My life was now intertwined with his, and we resolved never to let our bond wane. Though my love for Juan increased and became greater than any romantic love I had thus far experienced, I wanted to keep it defined as a friendship because I feared putting such a beautiful thing at risk.

After the Joshua experience, I now knew that I could not mix sex with friendship, so I spoke with Juan about this. We drew healthy boundaries, and the bond grew even more. Through him, I began to experience the meaning of unconditional love in which I could love another, and be loved, without any possessiveness or self-seeking. I realized that Juan was an intensely loyal person. In the first months of our friendship, I realized that he would remain in my life. Time would reveal the extent to which he would become God's gift.

My friendships were growing, and through them, I learned the meaning of unconditional love, love without drama, and a way of loving myself while loving the other person. I decided that I would not date for one year as I focused on friendship. Friendship was a healthy experience, and I thus began constructing the life for myself that I had looked for in others.

By the time my birthday arrived in February, I had a group of quality, loving friends who filled my house and added to my life.

As my friendships grew, so did my sense of peace. From the depths of sorrow and hurt, I was now enjoying my life and looked forward to the time I could spend with those friends who were becoming like family. They cared about what transpired in my life, as I did in theirs. I had my heart back.

Part III: Lessons on Friendship

My experience confirmed my belief that friends could become like family because I was lucky enough to have built lasting bonds with Thomas, Reed, Juan, and others. I didn't repeat the unhealthy patterns that had defined some of my romantic relationships. These friendships became like a "school" of healthy love that I could bring into the other parts of my life. If I found myself overly self-critical, I would ask myself whether I would say this to my friend. As I reflected on my romantic relationships, I asked myself whether I would behave this way with a friend or accept this behavior from a friend. These healthy friendships, then, became a guidepost to recognize healthy and unhealthy behavior.

During my adolescence, I longed for a closer family unit, especially after my mother passed away. I began to experience the permanency and sense of family for the first time since my childhood. I became comfortable in telling Thomas and Juan that I loved them. I revealed more of myself and found myself valued for who I was, as I learned to appreciate friends for who they were, faults and all. This love felt calm, peaceful, and sure.

Building friendships, however, was not the product of spontaneous generation. I had to devote time and energy to each friendship because they are living things. Just as a plant only grows when it has food and water, these friendships required time and energy to flourish. I started to put in the time by seeing closer friends regularly and keeping in touch with those I cared about. In time I recognized the fruit of this work as my life grew bigger to include others' lives.

By building new friendships and cultivating old ones, I began to build bonds of affection and trust that had sometimes been lacking in my romantic connections. Love without expectations was refreshing, and soon these friends, especially Thomas and Juan, became my second family. These attachments filled me with gratitude and with the certainty that love could grow and endure.

198

Chapter 7: Actions and Words

No wound is worse than counterfeited love.
Sophocles

Beliefs:
  A man reveals himself through his words.
  Love must be proven by sacrifice.

Part I: Risking Again

During this year of building friendships, I was contacted on Facebook by one Darnell from New York. He heard about the story of my time in the seminary and said that he valued that spiritual aspect in my life; he asked if we could keep in touch. His photos showed him to be a huge, muscular, handsome man, but I was thinking only of friendship. He agreed.

When he began asking to speak on the phone to bring our connection to a different level, I hesitated. I wasn't sure what his intentions were. Was he looking for a friend, sex, something else? I put off the phone conversations until I felt comfortable.

When we did talk, Darnell was full of compliments. "I love your voice! You sound so masculine." It seemed like he was more focused on the sound of my voice than on the content of our conversation. But this opened a door, and we began to speak regularly.

Darnell described his experience with someone he was seeing. "I don't know, Mark. I feel the storm is on the horizon. Why is love so complicated? Can we talk about that?" We talked, and I told him about my history and why I took a year off from dating.

"I want to develop a good relationship with myself," I told him one evening. "I want to surround myself with good friends, quality people, but mostly, I don't want to look to someone else to make me happy." I recounted my previous experience with Joshua, who Darnell knew by reputation as it turned out.

Weeks and months passed as my affection for Darnell grew. We seemed to share a spiritual connection and a sense of disillusionment in certain aspects of gay life. He said he wanted something more. "I can come out to California sometime," he told me. "I have some clients out there, and then we can meet." I wasn't ready for this step, but I told him I would let him know.

I was going to Germany in September and would meet European friends there for a two-week trip. I would put this communication with Darnell on hold and focus on other areas of my life.

Though Darnell's interests seemed to parallel my own, I was cautious, given my experience with Joshua. Though I sensed that Darnell was interested in more than friendship, I kept the boundary clear. By focusing on friendship, this year had been so good; I was reluctant to put myself at risk in another relationship. My trip to Europe came at just the right time.

Part II: Berlin: Friendship and Expectations

Berlin is a renaissance city, with the most daring architecture that I had seen in one place anywhere. The museums were incredible, the people were friendly and helpful, and the cultural life was rich. I loved Berlin, and each day was fuller than the one before.

As I was enjoying the city and the friends I met there, one morning without warning or apparent cause, I awoke with a desire to meet Darnell. I imagined it not as a date but a meeting of friends. I texted Darnell from Germany. "I am ready to meet up if you are." He replied that he would see me in a few weeks.

I put this aside to be present with friends and enjoy this glorious city of Berlin, but soon it was time to depart for California.

I had been planning a trip up to San Francisco after my return from Germany. It was the time of the "Folsom Street Fair," a weekend in September during which San Francisco celebrates the gay leather scene. It was a street fair with booths, a dance, and other events, all with a leather theme. Juan, two other friends, and I thought it would be fun to go and see what it was all about.

Part III: Ready for Love?

The four of us were still in the final planning stages for our San Francisco trip when Darnell arrived a few days later; the plan was to meet at his hotel and then go out to dinner. On my way over, I wondered whether this were friendship or something else. I became aware that I had no strong feelings; I neither looked forward to this meeting, nor dreaded it. I didn't feel particularly sexual, nor did I have any expectations. I decided to simply be open.

I only began to feel nervous when I got out of the elevator and approached his room. Before I could knock, the door opened; a man with a shaved head, heavily tattooed arms, a handsome face, and a smaller build than in his photos, greeted me. "Mark!" he said as he hugged me. "Do you like what you see?" he asked. I hesitated as I nodded, though I had expected a much bulkier man. The photos he had posted online taken had been taken when he was on steroids and was about fifty pounds heavier.

I had made a reservation at a nice Italian restaurant nearby where Darnell and I could get to know each other. One of the first things he said was that he was now single and that his relationship was over. I wasn't sure where this was heading, but I found him an attractive man: masculine, a sense of integrity, and a certain spirituality.

We hit it off that evening, and Darnell asked if we could see each other the following day and spend the night together. We were crossing from friendship into dating without any forethought. I said," Yes."

If this was to be a date and not just a friend, I wanted to introduce Darnell to my friends. I wanted him to get to know what type of people were in my life, and I was also open to input my friends had given my clouded judgment about men in the past.

I introduced Darnell to my best friend Thomas, who had a positive impression of this lively, articulate man. Darnell worked in sales, and it was apparent that he felt extremely comfortable dealing with people.

That night after dinner, we had sex; it was not the most intense sexual encounter I ever had. Darnell was more of a "beached whale," waiting for me to do the work. His kisses were neither deep nor romantic; in fact, his passion seemed to lag. Nonetheless, I enjoyed the experience because I was interested in Darnell, the man, and not just Darnell the body.

The next day I invited my close friend Juan to come over, and we all planned to go to lunch. Over the meal, Darnell spoke a lot about his devotion to his daughter, who was living in Florida and raised by his ex-wife. "I just can't get over the fact that she is part of me, another part of me out there," he repeated. When the day was over, Juan said to me. "I don't think Darnell has room for a relationship with his traveling job and his daughter; I think you would always be in third place."

I had a previously scheduled trip to Florida the following month to visit my friend Phillip. "Let me know the dates, and I will meet you there," Darnell suggested. He seemed to be as interested in me as I was becoming in him, so we made a Florida plan.

"See you in a few weeks," I said to Darnell as he left for the airport, planting a kiss firmly on his lips. I then turned my attention to our leather adventure.

Though friendship seemed a safe harbor after my various relationships, the meeting with Darnell invited me to step beyond this boundary. There was a mutual attraction; he shared some of my interests, and his experience with healthy and unhealthy relationships mirrored my own. At the end of the year of friendship, I made a conscious decision to step once more into the dating world and get to know this man, Darnell.

The following week, friends Juan, Rex, Raymond, and I departed for the Folsom Street Fair in San Francisco. We attended the events and the street fair together, and our bonds of friendship grew. Toward the end of those four days, we didn't want to leave. It was Rex who remarked, "I could keep living this way with you guys always." My friends had indeed become like family.

Part IV: In Florida and Over My Head

I was in Florida the week following San Francisco, staying with my friend Phillip. Darnell made arrangements to fly down the following day. He needed to spend time with his daughter, he informed me, but we would plan some time together.

When Darnell arrived, he became completely immersed in his daughter and her teenage issues. I heard from him that same day. "I have to spend the day with Sofia, but I will see you in the afternoon." When afternoon arrived, I got another text: "I will meet you for dinner." Darnell showed up around 8:30, so the three of us, Phillip, Darnell, and I, went out to a restaurant. Though a bit late for Philip and myself, we tried to accommodate Darnell.

Darnell declined to sleep with me at Phillip's house but promised that we would be together the next night. Because Phillip was leaving town, we would have the place to ourselves.

I bought flowers and had a card waiting for Darnell when he arrived the following evening at about 9 p.m. "Oh, thank you so much, honey," he said as we embraced.

I had heated the Jacuzzi, and we went into the hot, swirling water to relax. Darnell recounted his childhood, his disappointment with his father, his strong attachment to his mother, and his struggle to accept his sexuality. This struggle led him to be discharged from the military, followed by a string of sexual experiences with women, his consequent marriage, and the birth of his child. He told me of his decision to tell his daughter that he was gay while she was still a little girl and his subsequent decision to leave his wife and young daughter because he needed to "start living my own life." His brothers turned against him on this issue, and he was alienated from them for some time.

None of this information triggered any red flags for me. My emotions for Darnell were already clouding my judgment.

We began to kiss and become aroused and soon found ourselves in Phillip's bed making love. Again, I seemed to be the one making most of the sexual effort.

"What do you like to do sexually?" I asked him afterward.

"When I know you better, we will talk about that." His response took me aback. Why this hesitancy when we were already in bed having sex? I was perplexed. He did open up, however, about his drug use. "My friends give me a tough time because Ecstasy does not affect me at all. I don't like marijuana. I like poppers sometimes," he continued. "What gets me going and feeling loving is Crystal. I'd love to do Crystal with you someday," he said.

I was shocked. I had already gone through Warren's Crystal addiction and didn't want to ever get near the stuff again. "How often do you use? When did you use last?" I asked, wondering about the repercussions of this revelation. "Oh, it's been a year and a half, maybe even two years. I have rarely used," he said. I believed his words. But I did not yet know how I would deal with this should the drug issue surface; I would not live that nightmare again.

We slept in late that next day because Darnell kept saying, "Just fifteen more minutes," from around 9 a.m. until noon. Once he was up and showered, he went off to spend the day with his daughter again; he promised that we would meet for dinner.

I spent that day alone and grew restless; I resolved that it would not be in Florida the next time I saw Darnell because his daughter seemed to require so much attention.

We met at a favorite Italian restaurant of Darnell's in the gay area of town that night. He was such a personable guy, I thought, as he asked the server about her family in France, her boyfriend in Florida, and her feelings about both. When a group of muscle men entered and sat down at a table across the room, after glancing over at us several times, Darnell leaned over and said that most in the gay community in Florida consider him to be aloof. Several of them were texting on their phones when Darnell also commented, "They are probably looking for hookups."

During the dinner, my newfound feelings for Darnell bubbled to the surface. I reached over and looked into his eyes as he gazed back. "I want you in my life for good, Darnell. There is something beautiful between us. Do you feel it?"

He squeezed my hand and replied, "Yes, I do." I felt so close to him at that moment that I wanted it to last forever.

Darnell was non-committal about when to see each other the following days. When I suggested that we rent a hotel room together to at least see each other at night, his reply was, "I will let you know." I understood that he had to put his daughter first, and I was adept at putting other people's needs before my own.

"He's a butterfly, Mark," my friend Phillip said. "That would drive me crazy. Why can't he just give you an answer so you can make your plans?" he said. I shrugged. Finally, around 4 p.m., Darnell texted me and told me to book the hotel for that night.

The hotel room was perfect. Around 7 p.m. Darnell texted, saying that he would be coming later and to go ahead and eat; I went to a nearby restaurant where I had a forgettable meal. He kept texting, "I'll be there in another hour," and when an hour passed, "I got delayed. I'm sorry. Another hour." By the time he did pull up, it was 11 p.m. He was full of apologies, and I was not irritated because his daughter had to come first, and I was the newcomer. "Can we go to McDonald's? Please, please, please?" he pleaded. We went and had some junk food. He was exhausted, so we lay in bed, kissed, and he was quickly off to sleep.

The next day was Darnell's last in Florida, and he had to make some work calls. "Do you want to book this room for tonight?" I asked.

"I'll let you know," was his non-committal answer.

"Family first," I said.

"You're wonderful. Men I've dated in the past didn't understand that." He then went his way, and I went back to Phillip's.

Later, Darnell texted that he would come by Phillip's

house at 5 p.m. and spend a little time that evening, but he would not stay over because his daughter wanted to bring him to the airport. Family first, I repeated to myself once more.

Darnell showed up late again. "You will meet my daughter, Mark. And I want you to meet Damian also, my best friend. Next time you come here, I will organize this better, so we have our place together." I followed him out to his car. "We'll see each other in a few weeks," he said, "either here in Florida, or California, or even New York." We kissed and said good night. As I went into my room and crawled into bed, I said to myself out loud, "It ain't gonna be in Florida, my friend," I pulled up my sheets and drifted off into sleep.

I believed in Darnell's words of love and affection, but his actions in Florida seemed to confirm what Juan said; his daughter and the other parts of his life would come first. Perhaps there was little room in his life for a relationship; there was little room in his schedule in Florida to spend time together. He said this was because his daughter needed time with him; though I understood this priority, I found myself in the uncomfortable situation of being on "stand by." This didn't work for me. My feelings for Darnell were growing as he invited me deeper into his life but always at some undefined future date.

Part V: The "L" Word

I returned to California, and after a few days, I got a text from Darnell. "Did you get my message on your answering machine?"

"No. Is everything OK?" I responded.

He answered, "It's all on the message." I became concerned. My mind started to spin as I imagined that he was dumping me on my answering machine. By the time I did get home, I was sure that was the case.

I pressed the "play" button: "Mark, I don't want you to be worried because I am OK, but I am in the hospital. They are just doing some tests. When we talk, I will tell you more."

When I did reach him on the phone, he explained that he had been taking Growth Hormone to build muscles, which interacted with a medication his doctor had prescribed, which had made his blood sugar so dangerously high that he was at risk of a stroke. He was being given insulin and was beginning to stabilize. "I will fly out there if you want," I offered.

"No, that won't be necessary. They will discharge me tomorrow. I'll be fine. But I wanted you to know because I don't want to keep anything from you," he said.

"Does your daughter Sofia know?" I asked.

"No, she will just worry herself to death. I don't want her to know."

Hours later, I called; he answered groggily, "Mark, is that you?"

"Yes, are you OK?"

He replied, "I was just dreaming about you. I dreamed you were sitting by my bed. I could feel you holding my hand, all this love coming from you, and you told me that I would be all right. It was as if you were here. By any chance, Mark, are you wearing yellow?"

I looked down at the shirt that I had thoughtlessly slipped on that day. "How did you know I was wearing yellow?" I asked in disbelief.

"You were wearing a yellow shirt when I saw you here. Take a picture of yourself and text it to me," which I did. "That's exactly how you were dressed in my dream! What does that mean?" he asked. I had no idea, but I hoped that it was some type of blessing on the relationship that we were building.

A few days after he was released from the hospital, Darnell asked if I would consider meeting him in Boston. "I want to spend time with you after that health scare. You are such a loving man," he said. I made arrangements for my flight.

It was November, and the weather in Boston should have been cold and unpleasant, but instead, it was sunny and warm. As we drove from the airport, Darnell explained that "I had to stop taking testosterone, so I may not be up for sex this weekend, but at least we can be together. I hope that is all right with you, Mark."

I squeezed his hand; "I'm just happy to spend time with you," I reassured him.

It was a Friday, and we had four nights together. Darnell had to be in Boston for work, which meant he had to make a five-minute appearance at a hotel conference. The rest of the time was ours to enjoy each other and explore the city.

"This is our bonding room," he said as he left the hotel one morning. Our emotional connection and comfort level seemed to be growing by the hour.

We spent the following day with my friend Reed, who was temporarily living near Boston. Reed was a good friend and an important part of my life, and I valued this opportunity in which all three of us could spend time together. As we sat for a pizza later that

210

day, I learned more about Darnell by listening to his conversation with Reed. "I like dancing because I like getting sexual on the dance floor," he explained to Reed. The conversation moved forward until, somehow, it arrived at piercings. "I used to have a Prince Albert," he stated, then turned to me and said, "You did not know that about me." I did not think that Darnell was the type to have his penis pierced with a metal ring. As I sat there listening, I realized that, in many ways, he was a stranger to me.

"Why did you do that?" I asked. "I dunno. I was with friends. They wanted to do it, so I did it, too. But I got rid of it after about six months," he continued. His personality was pieces of a puzzle that I couldn't yet fit together.

When we returned to the hotel room, Darnell was exhausted, so I offered to massage his back. I gave him a long rub, during which time we spoke of everything from our family upbringing to world religions. When he turned over, I discovered that he was more ready for sex than he had anticipated. We began to kiss, and he looked deeply into my eyes as I said, "I love you, Darnell."

And he said, "I love you, Mark."

These words excited him even more as we dove into each other. Darnell seemed to be utterly present until he reached climax; after that, he closed his eyes and seemed to sink once more back inside of himself. I could see the walls go up and the distance appear.

The always chipper yet mysterious, Darnell emerged once more when he opened his eyes and said, "Wow! I didn't know that was in me," as he got up to shower.

"Would you feel comfortable if I use the 'L' word?" I asked Darnell the next day.

"Sure! If that's how you feel!" he replied, so I began telling him that I loved him from that day forward. I loved him yet did not yet know him. Was such a thing possible?

Before leaving Boston, we decided to begin calling each other daily.

My feelings were evolving for Darnell, but I was still not sure of his. He was so hesitant about expressing anything of himself that he sometimes reminded me of Joshua.

The process of getting to know each other could continue if we spent time together and communicated our feelings and emotions. Though I was more open than Darnell, I figured he needed more time.

While still in the airport, I texted him that I had two weeks off for Christmas. I asked if he was interested in spending some holiday time together. "Yes. Let's rent a cabin in the mountains somewhere," was his response.

During this time together, my feelings for Darnell grew even as my understanding of him remained blocked. He spoke little of his relationship history, and I had no secondary sources to ask about his past. I only knew what Darnell told me, and he told me very little. Yet my feelings grew to the point of telling him that I loved him; in reality, I loved the man he seemed to be. A man of commitment, integrity, no drama, friendly, and easy to bond with; this was the man that he presented himself to be through his words. I was guided by the belief that love is manifested through words, so I gave much weight to his words and little importance to his lack of initiative.

Part VI: Putting Him First

Once I was back in California, I realized that I was falling in love. I started writing him poetry that I began to send to Darnell almost every day.

Darnell's response to the poems was "Beautiful" or "Thank you." It perplexed me that he had no more words than that as I tried to express the emotions gushing out of my heart.

I did find a cabin in the Lake Tahoe region between Christmas and New Year's, and I was eager to reserve it because it was a busy time. "I'll let you know," Darnell said. "Sofia wants to spend New Year's with me, and Damian might come up. Let me work this out." I didn't push the matter further because it was up to Darnell, but his pattern of not committing to anything began to emerge once more.

Toward the end of November, I brought up the cabin rental to Darnell again with no decision in sight. "I will let you know by tomorrow, Mark. I want to do this." The next day he gave the green light. "I will send you a check for my part."

Darnell was not shy about asking me to do things for him, and I was willing because it made me feel closer to him. "Mark, I have a photograph of my daughter Sofia. It would mean so much to me if you could blow it up and have it framed. If you can, send it to me overnight, and I will reimburse you for it." I happily had the photo professionally prepared, searched for the frame, put it all together, and sent it off. It was a hefty sum, but I was happy to be part of something between Darnell and his daughter; it felt like I was being invited to participate in that sacred relationship. He also asked me to purchase and send him some protein powder and natural supplements. Though the cost was $600, Darnell assured me the check would be coming and was incredibly grateful. He called to say, "Thank you so much. I won't ask you to do anything else for me. A friend of mine asked me whether I could get that protein supplement for him. I didn't say anything, but I thought to myself, 'I'm going to have to talk with my husband.' But we don't have to deal with that now. I just want to thank you for helping me." I liked the term "husband," which seemed to confirm that we were on the same page.

December arrived, and I let my family know that Darnell would be joining us the day after Christmas. The plan was for all of us to have brunch together before the two of us drove up to our cabin in Lake Tahoe. I had never introduced my family to someone I was dating before, so this was a big step. I asked Darnell what he thought about that. "I'm looking forward to meeting them. I can't wait!"

Darnell wrote me an email the following week about his financial difficulties. "Mark, I have to pay a lot of expenses this month for Sofia's graduation. Could I pay you the money I owe in January? But I understand if you have expenses, and if that doesn't work, I will find the money somewhere." I agreed to delay repayment. I didn't have a problem with this because, by this time, I started to believe that this man and I were becoming like family. Sharing financial difficulties and joys and experiences felt as if we were already in the committed relationship that I imagined; I did not yet have the perspective to realize that I was repeating the same pattern that I had with Rafael.

I was excited about this time together. I packed my bag over a week before leaving for Sacramento and forwarded the cabin information to Darnell in New York. His daughter and ex-wife were visiting him for a few days, so I cut back on the texting and phone calls. "Mark, are you alright? I haven't heard from you," Darnell texted me.

"Family time," I texted back.

"You're adorable," was his response. Then he called me from the subway: "Mark, we are on the subway, and I just want you to feel part of this. I'll talk with you later, honey." All was well, we were growing together, and we were sharing more of our lives.

When Darnell phoned me the next day, I sensed that something was bothering him; he seemed down but was hesitant to discuss it. Eventually, he opened up. "My boss called me, and my company is going public. Because of that, we are being audited. The good part is, if the company goes public, I will be a millionaire. But to make a long story short, they have reclassified personal, and business expenses, and they expect me to come up with over $20,000 by next week! That's crazy! I don't have the savings to pay that. What am I going to do?"

I broke in, "I'll front you the money."

There was a silence, then "Mark, you would do that? You didn't even skip a beat. I feel so…. let me call you back; I'm just so choked up." He later accepted the loan. "I feel like family with you; I feel so close to you now. We must take this slow because I want to do this right with you; Mark, your trust in me moves me so much. We will write this out, come up with a repayment schedule, and have it notarized. Would $2,000 a month be acceptable to you as payback, starting in January?" I agreed and wired him the money the next day.

I was entrusting Darnell with both my heart and my financial well-being.

I had rescued Rafael from financial difficulty but never had I put myself at such financial risk as I did now. Darnell needed rescuing, and I stepped to the front without pausing. Why did I do this? I held to a belief that love had to be proved through sacrifice and that Darnell would see the depth of my commitment and trust through this loan. I was also anticipating a relationship that did not yet exist between us. I wanted to imagine that it did; the words spoken by Darnell confirmed that it did. But we neither had the history nor the knowledge of each other to take that step. I had not yet learned this lesson, so I was destined to repeat it.

Just a few days before Christmas, the bottom fell out. "Mark, I have some tough news. It's not for sure yet; I'll find out tomorrow, but my boss said I might not be able to go to California between Christmas and New Year's. Something came up at work, and they are going to ask one of us to visit some of our clients to solidify our accounts. I'm so sorry." I was devastated.

I slept a little and tried to pray away this setback. With hope, I took his call the next day. "Mark, they did choose me. In a way, it's a good thing because it shows they have confidence in me. I really can't refuse; if I did, I would have egg on my face. I'll make it up to you. I will work it out so that we can have some time together before you go back to school." He wasn't coming. The cabin had to be canceled. The brunch was off. My heart was crushed.

I put the cabin on hold for an undetermined

future date with Darnell and told my family about his predicament. We decided to proceed with the family brunch anyway, but I would shorten my stay and return to Los Angeles, hoping that I would see Darnell.

With a heavy heart, I flew up to Sacramento; I was pleased to see my family but sad that it would be without the man I loved.

I checked into the hotel that I had reserved for Darnell and me and settled in. It was late afternoon on Christmas day, and I would meet my parents and sister later that evening for a nice dinner at a restaurant on the other side of town. I lay on my bed and texted Darnell, "I'm here in Sacramento and thinking of you."

He responded later, "Thinking of you, too. I'll call you later."

There were few restaurants open on Christmas in Sacramento, but my parents found a great one: candlelit, white tablecloths, dark woods, delicious food. But I was distracted, keeping my eye on my phone that I placed next to my plate. While my parents, sister, and I caught up on family affairs, my eyes kept glancing at my phone. "Sorry, I'm a bit distracted," I apologized. "I was just hoping to hear from Darnell tonight," and as I finished these words, the phone rang. I grabbed it, excused myself, and flew out the door.

"Merry Christmas, Mark," was Darnell's greeting. "How is the family?" I proceeded to tell him of what had transpired thus far.

"When is Sharon coming? I miss Sharon. Tell her that her brother-in-law says hello!" He was referring to my other sister whom he had met on a previous visit; ever since this meeting, Darnell referred to Sharon as his "sister-in-law" or "the sister I never had." Sharon saw him more coolly, however, suspicious of his effusive affection.

The conversation was short, but the connection was made, and I was satisfied: I got to speak with Darnell on Christmas day. I was smiling when I returned to the table and was more present to my family than before. It was as if I got a fix of a drug and was fine until the next time.

I woke up early the next day. After going to the gym and washing up, I would meet my family at the restaurant for brunch. "Good morning and Merry Christmas again! I am thinking about you!" I texted Darnell, but I did not get any response. He is sleeping late, I thought. When I got my workout and shower done, I sent him another text: "Heading over to brunch. Can I call you first?" Again, no response. At my parent's house, I was bothered by Darnell's silence.

There were twenty of us at a long table at a local restaurant about half an hour later, and I ended up sitting in the middle of a group of friends of my parents whom I didn't know. I took a photo of family and friends, and I texted it to Darnell. I then called him, but he didn't pick up. It was strange. I wondered whether Darnell felt the sense of loss that I did. Toward the end of our meal, I got a text. "Enjoy the clan, Mark. I can't talk now. I am heading to a movie with Damian. No reception on the subway; can only text. Enjoy."

I stepped away from the table to contemplate the message. My expectations and hurt rose to the surface. I didn't understand how he had time to get ready and leave the house to go to a movie with a friend but didn't have two minutes to make a call. Plus, he knew that this brunch had been planned around him. Why would he not call? I shook my head. I could not control it, but it hurt me. I returned to the table and went through the motions of the brunch, just wanting it to be over, wanting to get back to my room, to pack my bags, and to return home to Los Angeles.

The rest of the Sacramento trip was a blur until I got on the plane to return home. There was a message from Darnell on my cell phone when I landed. "Mark, this is Darnell. I wanted to make sure you got home safe. Call me."

His concern surprised me, so I returned his call. "Hi, Mark. I just wanted to make sure you got in your house safe. So why don't you keep me on the phone as you drive home." We spoke softly as I drove, recounting to him the last twenty-four hours of my trip. "I just pulled up, and everything looks fine, but I'll let you know when I get inside," I reassured Darnell. I went up the stairs. "Everything is OK; thanks for being concerned," I told him. I bid him good night, but I was confused. The signals I was getting from him were all mixed up, and neither my heart nor my head could make sense of it.

I was beginning to realize that my belief that love is manifested through words no longer served me. Darnell's' actions and choices spoke most clearly and signaled where his heart was and what his priorities were. But I still could not distinguish words and actions, and both were so cluttered that I was confused. I started to live on the hope that his words were true. But I had few facts to support this hope.

Part VII: Putting My Heart on Hold

Not surprisingly, Darnell was unwilling to plan

to spend time together before I returned to work. His explanation sounded reasonable: because his daughter needed him, but his promises to make it up to me began to ring hollow.

New Year's arrived, and Darnell said he would stay home that night and call me. I made no plans because I knew I would just be thinking of Darnell. I decided to watch a movie, cook myself a nice dinner, and wait for Darnell's phone call around 9 p.m. my time.

I felt I was walking an emotional tightrope; so much of my sense of well-being depended on how Darnell responded. If he did call tonight, my New Year's celebration would be complete; if not, I would be devastated.

He did indeed call, to my relief. Did I realize how much I was putting myself at risk?

I started classes, and I still had no date to see Darnell again, nor had I received a check for the monies due. On the matter of getting together he remained elusive, but on the matter of the money he asked if he could begin payments in February. I agreed but was growing suspicious.

As the weeks passed, I realized that Darnell was becoming more a memory than reality; I voiced this to him one day. An avalanche of emotion began, which I was unable to stop.

"You're frustrated with me, Mark. I have to think whether I can give you what you want," was the response he gave that Friday afternoon. I began to feel that our dating relationship was over. This seemed to be confirmed by what he said in a subsequent phone call. "I want to move slowly. I don't want us to date exclusively." This was a strange request. I recalled a

220

story Darnell had told me about someone he had been dating in Chicago who, when he proposed to Darnell that they date non-exclusively, Darnell ended the relationship. Now he was offering the same to me.

My emotional spiral increased as I realized what was happening. "Mark, Darnell couldn't commit to getting a haircut, let alone to you! He abandoned his daughter!" my best friend Thomas commented.

"Darnell, I cannot keep someone as my priority if I am only their option," I told him. "Mark, I don't see it that way. You are my priority. I have been crying this afternoon. I want you in my life." His feelings seemed sincere, yet what he was proposing confused me.

The phone calls went back and forth that entire day until I told him that evening, before meeting some friends for dinner: "Darnell, it's OK. I will be all right. Whatever you decide is fine." I thus wanted to let him off the hook to walk away; at least I would know where I stood.

About an hour later, my friend Phillip, who had known Darnell for years, called. I recounted the whole miserable weekend experience. "Mark, look what he is saying. He loves you. I've seen Darnell come further with you than he has with anyone else. He just feels this is all moving too fast for him. He wants the option to date other people; it is just to slow this down, but I don't think he'll date anyone else. I've seen him in the past in these situations; when he dates someone, he focuses on them. This is just his way of slowing down, not breaking this off. I think if you give him that option, Darnell will come around, and when he does come around, he will rock your world." I wanted to believe Phillip's words, so I told Darnell that we could move more slowly and see what happens.

We were in the habit of speaking every evening, but this soon stopped. Darnell said he needed space, so I let him take the initiative to contact me. We spoke little during that time, which perplexed me more. I thought we had decided to date non-exclusively, but now it seemed we were not dating at all. He surprised me with a call one day as I was leaving work: "I'm on my way to seeing a movie with some friends. I just wanted to see how you were doing. How is your heart, Mark?" I told him that I missed him. "Mark, I want to tell you something unsolicited. I adore you. That's the truth." Though his words were affectionate, they rang empty.

Part VIII: Ignoring My Heart

I was willing to sacrifice my peace of mind to hold onto this relationship. I was still unable to step back and ask myself the simple question: was this relationship good for me or not?

I had been planning to go to Rome in March and invited Darnell to come on several occasions, but he constantly changed the subject. I decided to go by myself and meet Phillip, who would be in Rome at the same time. This trip became a benchmark for me. If I did not see Darnell before this trip, then I would end this relationship. I would hold out till March.

I heard from Darnell sporadically and at unexpected times. One afternoon he texted me: "Mark, the Jets are playing. Pray that they win and make it to the Super Bowl." It was odd because I hadn't heard from Darnell in five days; this was his only communication? I didn't answer. He texted me a few more times. He then called, so I picked up. "Mark, are you OK? I texted you about the Jets, and you didn't respond. At first, it made me mad. I just wanted to let you know I was thinking about you." He hung up. I scratched my head.

It was now early February. I called him and made it as clear as I could that I needed to see him before going to Rome. He promised that it would happen if it were that important to me.

On my birthday, I had some close friends over for a lasagna dinner; Darnell had called in the morning and promised he would call me again, but I didn't believe it, so I was not surprised when the call didn't arrive.

Though my heart was being taken for a ride, I had made the choice to be involved with this man emotionally and financially. Though I couldn't make sense of the conflicting signals coming from Darnell, the voice of my heart was clear: this was not good for me. I had little serenity, was in emotional turmoil and on the brink of financial disaster. I still felt that I didn't have enough information to figure this situation out because Darnell had been so guarded. His choices spoke more clearly, however. I was at sea and needed to get back to shore. I was setting my trip to Rome as my deadline since this was a way of getting my life back, one way or another.

Part IX: Falling Apart

By mid-month, I still hadn't received the promised February payment from Darnell, and things seemed to be getting stranger; he started to communicate with me only by text and declining to talk by phone. The exception was Valentine's Day when he called and said, "Mark, I wanted to wish you a happy Valentine's Day. If your friends ask, you can now say that I called." These were his final words.

I had some skin cancer removed the following week, and while there, the doctor found three more sites. I hadn't dealt with cancer before, so I was worried. When I returned home, I texted Darnell. "Just got back from the doctor. He gave me some upsetting news. Can we talk?"

Darnell texted back, "Can't talk now. What did he say?" He insisted on texting and said he was not free to talk. Other friends had phoned in their support that day, yet Darnell did not. His actions were speaking clearly.

I had to get back to a healthy lifestyle that did not revolve around Darnell; I knew this. Though my heart felt like scar tissue, I sought out my friends, went to the gym, tried to focus on work, and took care of myself. I would not contact Darnell, I decided, because the anticipation before and the disappointment after every attempted contact were destroying me. One day I went to the gym and focused only on the physical effort when, unexpectedly, a text from Darnell arrived. In it, he relayed to me that he would call me after I returned from Rome. Because my trip was not for another month, I wondered if this was his way of severing our ties.

I worked on an email to Darnell in which I asked him a simple question. I already knew the answer, but I wanted him to say it: Do you want to date me or not? The answer came clearly: "Mark, I am not emotionally available for a relationship, but we can see each other if there are no strings attached."

I read these words and realized what I needed to

do: I needed to take control of my life and my heart. I wrote to Darnell that I was stepping out of this situation since it just wasn't good for me.

That was it. The relationship was over, and my heart could begin to heal. We just had to resolve the money situation, and that would be the end.

After several days, I received several long texts from Darnell in which he seemed to backtrack on his earlier position. "Mark, I just need to get my head straight here. Go and experience life and love. Just know that I will still be here." I was getting mixed signals once more, just as I had from the beginning. But I could not get on that emotional roller coaster again.

Darnell made no mention of the $20,000 he had borrowed. He had asked me not to mention the loan to anyone, but now circumstances had changed. I felt vulnerable and hurt, so I sought counsel with friends. I still had not received a payment from him. I decided to make a payback proposal based on the verbal agreement that we had way back in December. I wrote Darnell and asked that he begin paying back the loan at the rate of $2,000 a month, starting the following month, which would be May. The answer I got called into question the real character of this person I thought I loved.

"Mark, you know my financial situation. We had agreed that I would just pay you what I can and when I can. You can't change our agreement. I told you that I had to pay for Sofia's graduation and then her college. But look, I'll send you four or five hundred dollars a month starting the end of June. That's what I can budget for, and that's what we agreed on."

It surprised me because we had never discussed a

June starting date nor a mere $500 a month. Who was this person?

The ongoing debt would continue to bind me to Darnell, which was not suitable for my emotional life. What leverage did I have? I finally consented to the $500 a month, figuring that something was better than nothing.

"I will only communicate with you if there is a matter regarding the monies owed. I promised to pay you off completely beginning at the end of June," he said. I hoped that would be the last word from him. I felt like a victim because I was now financially dependent on Darnell.

Feeling deceived, used, and ashamed, I eventually revealed the whole story to my friends. Juan offered me emotional support, often inexplicably showing up at just the right time. "Something told me that you needed some company today," he would say as I opened the door. I had other friends who offered their ear, but I was getting tired of talking of my heartache after some weeks in this state. It was time to focus on my trip to Rome and begin to heal.

Wanting information and trying to figure out what was happening between Darnell and me only prolonged the pain. I had enough information from my direct experience of how destructive this relationship was to my emotional life and finances. Sometimes trying to figure something out prevents one from doing something about it. Other people can remain a mystery, but my experience of them is clear. Listening to my experience became an essential step in my healing process.

By not paying back the money as promised, Darnell

revealed and confirmed the person that he always was: unable to make a commitment and carry it out. I knew this from his family history and behavior, but I still moved forward; this was my role. Joshua and Darnell had the same mindset or mental illness, yet I was attracted to both. At the end of this experience, I hoped that I had learned my lesson that past patterns often predict future behavior and that one's heart is revealed more by what one does than what one says. And for this lesson, I was grateful.

Chapter 8: Rome, Cancer, and Blessings

There is nothing noble about being superior to some other man. The true nobility is in being superior to your previous self.
Hindu Proverb

Beliefs:
My emotional well-being depends on another.
Cancer is the end of hope.
Trials reveal true friends.
Being a victim is a choice.

Part I: Healing in Rome

I always found myself healed and embraced when I went to Rome, so I counted the days until my departure: seeing friends and meeting up with Phillip gave me something to look forward to. I hoped that the experience would mitigate this constant pain I had in my chest.

The city kept its promise. Rome seemed more like a living person than a collection of buildings and individuals. Its personality permeated and filled me. My visit was before Easter; I could sense both the solemnity and the impending celebrations in the air, the food, the people, and even in the weather. I could feel waves of healing, and I stopped in more than one church asking that my heart, now in pieces, might be made whole sooner rather than later.

My faithful friend Stefano suggested we drive down to Naples. Stefano had known me since my seminary days, so we had no secrets. We arrived in that chaotic but wonderful city and stayed in a four-star hotel for less than a hundred bucks a night next to the historical section.

On our arrival, we were eager to get unpacked and get a taste of the city. We walked a few blocks until we came upon store after store selling Nativity set figurines. Some were of average quality, but most were amazing. We continued through the dark streets, crossing paths with lively, laughing Neapolitans, passing crowded pizzeria after pizzeria and silent baroque churches. I stopped to take a picture of one, so typically Naples: a beautiful church with a baroque marble façade and a mountain of garbage in front. It was a city of contrasts.

Our trip's focus was to be the archeological museum, but we first made our way to the famous cathedral the following day. The church held the remains of the beloved saint of Naples, Saint Januarius. The baroque church was truly awe-inspiring, but I was distracted by something in my heart. I needed to get it off my chest. I touched Stefano's arm. "I'm going to confession, and I'll be back in a minute."

What weighed most on me was the sorrow of these past months concerning my relationship with Darnell; somehow, I wanted to put this in God's "orbit." So, I knelt in the confessional and explained to the priest, in my best Italian, what happened in these past months. As I spoke, tears ran down my face, which turned to sobs. I felt betrayed by Darnell on all levels, emotionally and financially. But what part had I played? I tried to articulate this to the priest, and he caught on immediately. "The commandments aren't for God. He doesn't need them. They are for us, for our protection," he began. "God doesn't want you to be like this, so hurt and unhappy. The commandments are for us, not for God. What is the first commandment? To not place any gods before Him. But what does this mean? It means that if we place our sense of well-being in another person, we put ourselves at great risk. God wants you to be happy. Don't forget that." Opening my heart in that sacred space somehow made me feel absolved; God was more involved in my healing than before. I wiped my eyes, blew my nose, got up, and Stefano and I enjoyed the rest of the day together.

The priest's advice made sense, and his words remained with me for the rest of my trip. Making my feeling of well-being reside in someone else, letting someone else determine how I felt about myself, put me at risk. Hadn't I always done that in romantic relationships? Losing my sense of self, making it all depend on the other person, happiness consisting of measuring their response to my love? This was my wake-up call because my heart could not go through this again.

By the time I completed my trip to Rome, I felt I was on the road to healing; the turning point was in Naples' cathedral.

Part II: The Big "C"

When I returned home, I needed to keep some

previously scheduled medical appointments. My doctor sent me to an oncologist because I had some strange readings on a blood test that could indicate cancer, but most probably did not. Though I was nervous leading up to the appointment, I doubted it was cancer.

The oncologist explained that they would need to take a biopsy because that was the only way to know if cancer cells were present. "The levels in your blood are slightly elevated, which is not extreme, but neither is it normal. Higher levels can indicate cancer, but also many other things, so not to worry."

The day of the biopsy arrived, the tissue samples were taken, and the oncologist said he would call me with the results in a few days. "You're going to be fine. They will not find anything," friend after friend assured me. I began to think this myself, thereby avoiding the catastrophic thinking I was prone to.

When the doctor did call a few days later, I was stunned. "Mark, I am sorry to tell you that we did find some cancer cells in one of the samples. We caught it early, but if you don't do something about it, you will have future problems. You will not die from this if treated. I would recommend you choose either radiation or surgery in the next six months. We can meet again and discuss your options." I thanked him and hung up the phone. I was alone in my classroom. I would have to deal with my students shortly. But I sat back in my chair. "I have cancer," I said to myself in disbelief.

By the time I got home from work, I had mentally compounded my challenges all in one lump: cancer, broken heart, financial ruin. Later that evening, I received a call that my father had taken a fall and was in rapidly declining health. I felt overwhelmed.

Because my mother had passed away from cancer when I was a child, I held onto the belief that cancer was the end of hope. As soon as I was diagnosed, I realized that this belief would not serve me. I had some tools by this time, so I reached out to those friends I trusted to gain perspective. I also used my spiritual tools of prayer, mediation, and going to more Al-Anon meetings. These tools helped me realize that I could only deal with one situation at a time. I would focus on overcoming cancer first.

As far as Darnell's debt, I wondered if my cancer diagnosis might move him into paying me back in full. A mutual friend asked if he could reveal my condition to Darnell, and I agreed. Following this, I sent him a text: "I have cancer and have to go through treatment to fight it. I need the money returned as soon as possible."

Darnell's response was immediate and revealing. "Don't you have health insurance?"

Though the cancer diagnosis was devastating, the disease of my mind could take a more significant toll. If I gave up before even starting to fight cancer, I was already finished. Feeling surrounded by challenges, I reached out for those new spiritual and emotional tools that I was developing. It became clear that I would have the strength to face the challenges of cancer, finances, worry, and disappointment, with a force from within that my spiritual toolbox would sharpen and magnify.

Part III: Choosing Friends Unwisely

I kept a weekly taco date with two friends, Rex and

Tiago. It was the beginning of a positive friendship with these men. We shared one another's lives, triumphs, and challenges within an atmosphere of support and affection. Tiago took a particular interest in my heartache over Darnell, whom he had met on one of his visits. "Have you started to date anyone else, Mark? That could help you get over this." I did go on a date, and Tiago kept encouraging me to continue. He and Rex expressed concern about my cancer diagnosis, but Tiago seemed particularly concerned about my dating other men as a means of emotional recovery.

I heard that Darnell was heading to Los Angles, and he confirmed this in a text: "I don't know if you want to see me, but I will be in L.A. next weekend and would be happy to meet with you if you want." Why did he keep trying to contact me? Darnell was confident in his ability to manipulate. If he could speak to me, he probably believed he could bring me around to admitting that somehow, I was in the wrong here, and that it was I who had misunderstood him, and that he was abiding by the decisions of our financial agreement all along. I was not interested in being manipulated, so I ignored the text.

Darnell also contacted my close friend, Thomas, asking to meet with him while in town. Thomas accepted. I asked him to try to push Darnell to pay me back.

As the weekend approached, I became more nervous and did not want to bump into Darnell while he was here. I shared my fears with Rex and Tiago at our weekly taco dinner. Rex thought it unlikely that I would see Darnell; Tiago remained silent on the subject.

The weekend came and went without news about

Darnell, and Thomas didn't hear from him either.

A few days later, I received a text from Darnell: "Mark, I was in Los Angeles and was sorry not to see you. I thought of you often." I read this message with skepticism because this man was an expert at faking affection. My misgivings were confirmed a few days later.

Lots of personal information flows along the gay grapevine, and I heard that, while in Los Angeles, Darnell had extended his stay because he had a sexual and romantic interest with someone in town. He also attended a dance for gay pride that weekend, which I heard about, but could not afford. "What a shithead!" a friend of mine commented when I shared this.

I was still not free of Darnell because this information upset me. I had an emotional reaction as I realized that I had not meant anything to this man. I was simply one more notch on his belt, one more person he used for emotional and sexual affirmation, as well as financial gain.

A few days later was our weekly taco date, but Rex texted me while I was on the way, saying he could not make it. It would be only Tiago and me. There was lots of traffic, so the drive took me longer than expected, and I began to reflect on Darnell's weekend in Los Angeles. I then began to think about Tiago: his interest in my relationship and dating, his past comments about Darnell hinting at his attraction, his silence when I brought up Darnell's visit the prior week. Something wasn't right; I could sense it. It began as a feeling, continued as a hunch, and by the time I reached the restaurant, it was suspicion.

I met Tiago on the street, and he kissed me. We sat

down at a table and ordered sodas. "How was your week? How are you, Mark?" he asked. I paused.

Then I spoke: "I don't know if I should bring this up or not; it's just that something is bothering me."

Tiago broke in, "What? Now you have to say it!"

I took a breath. "OK. Tiago, have you been in touch with Darnell?"

Tiago looked at me with shock, then said, "Yes."

My heartbeat faster; I was surprised, but I went further. "Did you see Darnell this past weekend?"

Again, Tiago replied, "Yes."

I dared to continue. "Was it you that he had the fuck fest with this past weekend?"

Tiago looked down and said, "Oh, you heard about that?"

I was stunned. As I rose from the table, I said, "I feel betrayed!" I then walked to my car and drove home.

My hands were shaking. I felt betrayed on two fronts: by Darnell and by another man I thought was my friend. My anger grew as I drove, wondering if Tiago had been undermining my efforts to get my money back from Darnell. He could well have told him that my cancer was at the beginning stages, that I would be fine, and that I didn't need the money. I had no idea what kind of information Tiago had passed to Darnell, but betrayal was foremost in my mind.

Driving home stunned, I called Juan, who was also friends with Tiago. "What a scoundrel, to be masquerading as your friend all along!" But I still could not wrap my mind around what had just happened.

When I got home, I called Thomas, who had been the most connected with Darnell among my friends. I told him what just took place. "Well, Darnell got caught with his pants down! Who he has now been revealed to everyone."

As Thomas and I spoke, he received a text from Darnell: "Thomas, please call me now. I need to talk with you desperately!"

Thomas laughed. "He is trying to do damage control," he said.

When the emotion died down a few days later, I realized that this incident was a good thing. Darnell had been revealed for who he was, and I got rid of duplicitous Tiago. It felt like I was cleaning the house, and my emotions for Darnell were now dead.

A few days later, Darnell texted me and blamed me for the events. "Mark, you are creating all this drama. Stop it!" I read this message and wondered if this man was indeed out of his mind.

Whatever the character of Darnell or Tiago or anyone else, the time had come for me to stop being the victim. I was ready to take back my life.

Part IV: Victim No More

Juan coined a name for Darnell that stuck: "El Vampiro" or The Vampire. This described his modus operandi as well as his similarity to Joshua.

I needed to figure out a way to get control of my financial situation. I hired a lawyer and filed a lawsuit; we would force "El Vampiro" to settle, and then I could leave this behind me. "El Vampiro" refused and made his intention known that he would appear in court to fight me over the money owed.

As the months passed, heading into the hearing, I repeatedly thought about what I would say to him when we met. When the day of the trial arrived, however, my gut said to say nothing. I realized that no comment I came up with could change another person.

As I sat outside the courtroom waiting, "El Vampiro" walked up to look for his name posted outside the room. He had put on weight and didn't look healthy. As I sat waiting to be called into the courtroom, I felt peace coming from the certainty that I was doing the right thing.

The trial only lasted about forty minutes. Darnell argued that the court had no jurisdiction over him, being a New York resident, and his supporting argument was that there was no contract between us stipulating that the money had to be paid back. My lawyer produced numerous emails from him promising to repay. It was an easy judgment; the money must be paid back at once.

As we left the courtroom, I felt a weight lifted. No longer did I have to imagine what I would say to this person or how the trial might go. I felt no need to admonish him because I was no longer even angry. I finally felt free.

The whole experience had a surreal quality to it; here, I had to face in court the one I had thought was the man of my life, who was refusing to pay back all my life savings. But as I walked out to my car and drove home, I felt good about myself. I preserved the one thing that endured: my integrity. This made me feel proud of the man that I was finally becoming.

Part V: Lessons from the Vampire

To learn from an experience and avoid repeating

unhealthy patterns, it is necessary to look at one's role and not blame the other person for being who he/she is.

In my relationship with Darnell, some core beliefs that held me back from my happiness were being tested. I believed that love revealed itself more by words than actions; that love must be proven by self-sacrifice. I also thought that one's emotional well-being depends on another and that being a victim is a choice; all of these were like a hypothesis put to the test and conclusions reached.

One of the challenges of a long-distance relationship is that the only information one has about the other person comes from two sources: what the person says and what they do. Dating someone local has the advantage of having a third source: what the person's reputation is. Darnell articulated all those thoughts, values, and beliefs that guided my life and seemed to mirror what I was seeking. When I gave more weight to his words than to his actions, I found myself confused. But because I wanted to believe that he was the man that he appeared to be, I excused his actions and lack of initiative while the turmoil grew in my heart.

The role I played here was ignoring with my mind what I knew in my heart: that this relationship was not good for me. I didn't have to figure out why fire burned my hand before pulling it from the flame, yet I did want to figure out what was going on inside Darnell before removing my heart from harm. This belief that I needed to figure out a relationship before removing myself from harm's way was no longer serving me. My responsibility was to listen to that primary source of information that I could immediately access: whether this person was good for me or not.

The belief that love must be proven by self-sacrifice was ingrained since childhood as I tried to cope with witnessing my mother's declining health and then losing her battle with cancer. That other's needs come before my own was the natural course of events, and putting someone before myself was the proof of love. By loaning my life savings to Darnell, I repeated this pattern and confirmed my belief that love had to be proven by the financial risk that I put myself in. This belief no longer served me as I witnessed its consequences. The certainty of love didn't have to be proven through sacrifice but instead could be the product of building a history together. One cannot jump over this building process by making some ultimate sacrifice on behalf of the other. If I found myself again with someone I felt I had to prove my love to through a sacrificial offering, I could be sure that this was not love.

Before my trip to Naples, I conceived of religious rules as things I needed to go by to please my Higher Power. Somehow the rules were for God and not for me. When I walked into that confessional, this was turned on its head.

I would never consciously make another person or thing my God or Higher Power; I strove to live a spiritual life and didn't believe that another person or thing was my destiny. I realized that day in Naples that, though I was not deifying another person intellectually, I was doing so emotionally. Somehow my sense of well-being and feeling OK with my own life came to depend on how my relationship with Darnell was going. If things were well between him and me, then I felt good about my life. If things were confusing or bad, this influenced everything else. The priest's words opened my eyes to the risk I was putting myself in. The first commandment was for my good. I realized that it was not a contradiction to love myself and my Higher Power and that to love another is to love oneself first.

The relationship with Darnell was a difficult school to take lessons from because it impacted my emotional life and my financial stability. But what I could carry forward were tools that I could use to care for someone without doing for them what they can do for themselves. I learned that I could empathize with someone's problem, financial or otherwise, without trying to solve it. It also became apparent that actions are a clearer communicator than words. The simple question to myself, "Is this working for me?" can cut across all the confusion. Lastly, I remain grateful because, from this relationship, I learned that a healthy love for another could only flow from a healthy love of oneself.

Chapter 9: Epiphany: Forward

People are like stained-glass windows. They sparkle and shine when the sun is out, but when the darkness sets in their true beauty is revealed only if there is light from within.
Elisabeth Kübler-Ross

My cancer was in the initial stages, and I elected to have surgery as opposed to radiation. The surgery was scheduled for September first; I managed to keep my mind off it for months. But when the date arrived, I was frightened. What would be discovered once they opened me up? Even if all the cancer was removed, my body would function differently. I was still young, I still hoped for a loving relationship. Would this operation end that possibility? What about the side effects? My head was in turmoil.

"Baby, I can stay over with you the night before surgery, if you want. Then I'll drive you there," my dear friend Juan offered. I was grateful for his company that night. He held me until the morning, comforting me in his embrace. Juan was my family.

I was in a surprisingly peaceful sleep when the alarm rang at 4:30 a.m. Like a robot, I got out of bed, showered, and prepared to leave for the hospital. Another friend, Victor, was staying with me also, having volunteered to assist me for several weeks. "See you later today," I called out to Victor as we walked out the front door. I felt no emotion. "God, I put myself in your arms," was my prayer that morning.

We got into the car, and Juan and I held hands as we raced toward the hospital. We got there early, so we sat closely together. I was overwhelmed with fear as the nurse announced that I would be called in 15 minutes. The moments seemed like hours, and then the door opened again. "Mark, please come in for the preparation. Your friend can join you in a while." I squeezed Juan's hand, hugged him, and got up. He could see me in about 45 minutes. Once inside, I removed my clothes, got weighed, had my blood pressure and temperature measured; the nurse then shaved me in the surgical area.

I lay on the table, hooked up to the IVs when Juan came in, and sat down next to me. He took my hand as nurses came back and forth, giving me information, doing tests, attaching monitors. Then the anesthesiologist came and introduced herself and began to explain what would take place. I reached for Juan's hand. The fear was apparent on my face. I turned and looked at Juan. The anesthesiologist asked, "What are you scared of? Is it one thing?" Tears were streaming down my face, but I could not answer. "Is it just everything?" I nodded and gripped Juan's hand as firmly as I could. "You are going to be fine, just fine," she reassured me. "I will give you something to relax you. It will be like a strong Margarita," she said as she introduced a sedative into my bloodstream. I looked over at Juan, and the last thing I remember seeing was his tear-filled eyes.

I awoke to a smile. It was Juan looking down on me. "You made it, baby, and you are fine!" he pronounced. "The doctor told us that he got all the cancer!" After a few minutes, he said: "I'll let your sister come in," and I looked up and saw her above me, looking concerned.

"You are in the recovery room. They will put you in a regular room in an hour," I heard a voice say. I felt so much pain in my stomach area; I began to repeat over and over, "I want to go home! Please take me home!" A decision was made to keep visitors away until the evening because I was moaning in pain.

I must have fallen asleep because I was in a different room when I woke up again. I became aware of the faces around me. There was Juan, my loving and close friend. There was Victor, who had been in D.C. with me when I had my first experience of a relationship. Here was my sister who knew well the loss I experienced in my youth when our mother died. Next to her was Thomas, whom I met when I was still working at a church in Sacramento, and who was my best friend and mentor, with his partner, Reed, a profound man whom I called the "heart of West Hollywood." Ed, who had been in the seminary, and whom I met when I first moved to Los Angeles.

The faces moved from shadows to become more real. I blinked and looked around me repeatedly. Tears streamed down my face. "Are you alright?" Juan gently asked me. I couldn't speak any words; I could only weep.

I realized at that moment that the love that I had always sought, over and over again, in relationship after relationship, was already here. It was not only in those around me; it was already within myself.

Chapter 10: Final Lessons

What lies behind us and what lies before us are tiny matters
compared with what lies within us.
Ralph Waldo Emerson

My relationships and life events contain lessons that I was sometimes attentive to but other times suppressed until I was willing to listen. Becoming a student of life means becoming aware of the meanings behind things, and it would take many lessons for me to realize this. Wisdom is the product of experiences that have been reflected on, and with this wisdom, life can become fulfilling and joyful even when facing challenges.

At the end of this journey, I'm grateful for the joys and pains of searching for love in others because it eventually led back to me. I hope others might benefit from my experiences.

I am on the brink of a new relationship now, but it is different from the ones that came before. No longer is it driven by need or dependence or an emotional high. Instead, it is born from that certainty that we are as lovable to ourselves as we are to each other. The source of our bond is not that one person is the destiny of the other, but that we journey toward our destiny, beyond ourselves, together.

Milton Keynes UK
Ingram Content Group UK Ltd.
UKHW040726210924
448513UK00018B/386